A HISTORY *of* Charleston's HAMPTON PARK

A HISTORY *of* *Charleston's* HAMPTON PARK

KEVIN R. EBERLE

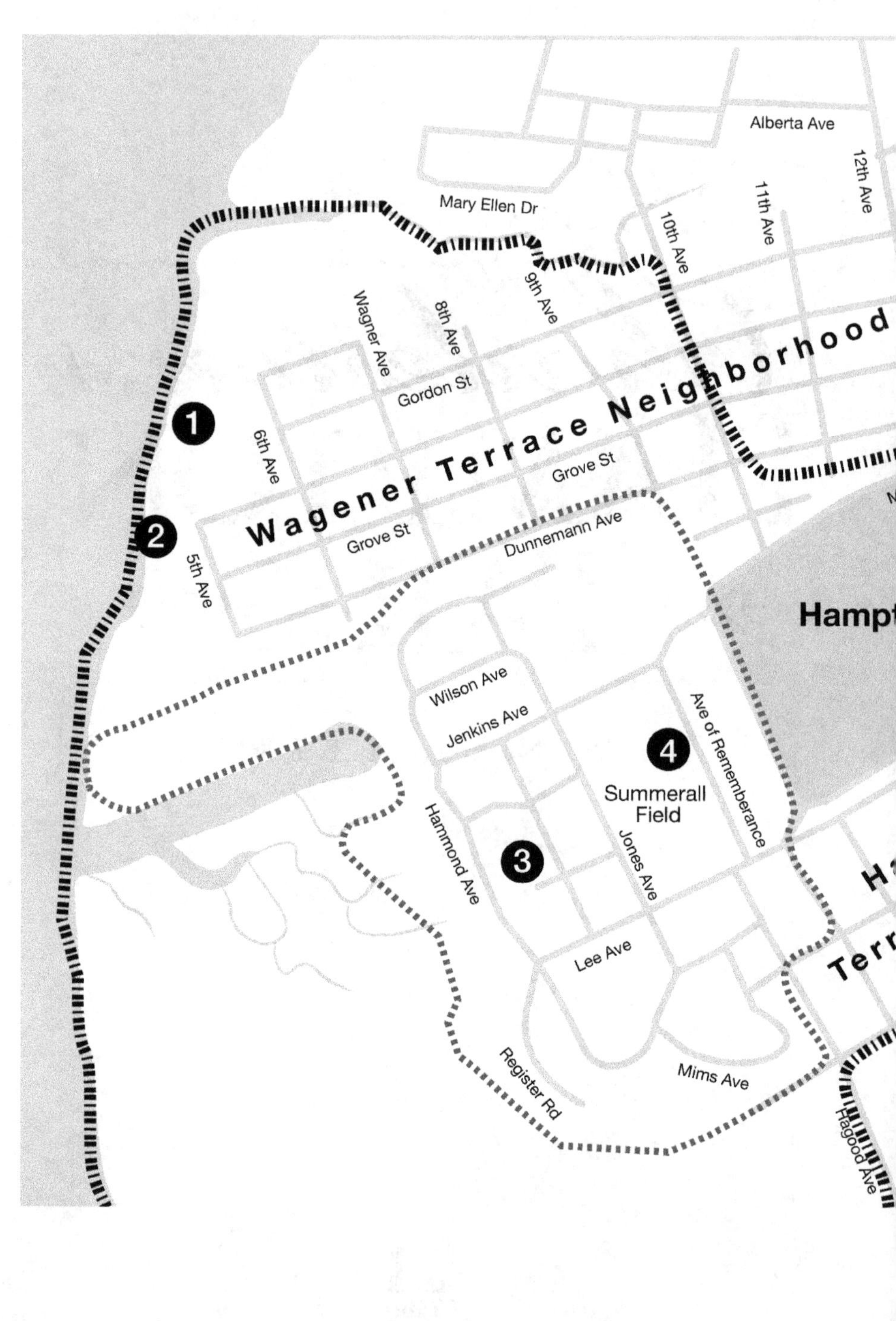

Alberta Ave
12th Ave
11th Ave
10th Ave
Mary Ellen Dr
9th Ave
8th Ave
Wagner Ave
Gordon St
Wagener Terrace Neighborhood
6th Ave
Grove St
Grove St
Dunnemann Ave
5th Ave
1
2
Hampt
Wilson Ave
Jenkins Ave
Ave of Rememberance
4
Summerall Field
Hammond Ave
3
Jones Ave
Lee Ave
Register Rd
Mims Ave
Hagood Ave
Terr

Orange Grove Plantation (approx.)
The Citadel Campus
1 Lowndes Grove Plantation House (after 1786)
2 Site of Gibbes' Landing
3 Indian Hill
4 Site of Orange Grove Plantation House (approx.)
Simon St
Septima Clark Pkwy
Meeting St
Rutledge Ave
King St
Huger St
Congress St
Moultrie St
Park
ighborhood
Race St
Sumter St
Rutledge Ave
President St
Ashley Ave
Coming St
Fishburne St

Published by The History Press
Charleston, SC 29403
www.historypress.net

Cover: The bandstand is an icon of Hampton Park. This postcard image from before 1925 shows the bandstand in its original location at the northern end of the Sunken Gardens. It has been moved twice since 1901.

First published 2012

ISBN 978.1.5402.3170.3

Library of Congress CIP data applied for.

Notice: The information in this book is true and complete to the best of our knowledge. It is offered without guarantee on the part of the author or The History Press. The author and The History Press disclaim all liability in connection with the use of this book.

Contents

ACKNOWLEDGEMENTS

The idea for this book occurred in early 2011, but its origins are much older. In 1995, I graduated from law school and returned to Charleston. I wanted to live in an old house, but houses in the historic lower peninsula were beyond the means of a new law firm associate. My focus turned to the upper peninsula—that area above the Septima P. Crosstown (Highway 17) that had neither decayed beyond my ability to restore nor been gentrified beyond my means. I quickly decided that Hampton Park Terrace was the ideal neighborhood, and by the spring of 1996, I had bought a solid, architecturally interesting house built in the summer of 1914.

I got involved with my neighborhood association and soon found myself authoring our monthly newsletter. Our tiny slice of Charleston was being nominated as a historic district on the National Register of Historic Places, and I used that as a taking-off point for a new column in our newsletter. Each month, I picked a house that interested me and did in-depth research on it. The resulting column was titled "Do You Know Your Neighborhood?" and was warmly received by my neighbors.

Over time, my research crept outward and started picking up our namesake park, Hampton Park. Over a decade, my files grew to include pages and pages of random notes about the park, but the only audience was me. Then, in 2010, I got an e-mail from fellow compulsive historian Valerie Perry. Valerie had been contacted about writing a history of Hampton Park, but she had to decline because she was already fully engaged in writing what would be released as her excellent first novel, *Upper King Street*. She gave my name as another possible source for the park's history, and within a few weeks,

I was hard at work organizing my stacks of research, lists of contacts and old images into what I hope will be both a useful resource and an enjoyable read.

As the writing of this book draws to a close, I have many people to thank. Valerie Perry deserves my boundless thanks and not just as the initial recommender of my services. She is a dear friend who has been an untiring sounding board for thoughts about this book and has enthusiastically responded to every topic I've raised with her. Her unflappable belief that Hampton Park is a special place that could sustain a book-length treatment is more responsible for this work than I can say.

There are also many groups and people who have been willing to go above and beyond in helping me research this book. I would be remiss if I did not call particular attention to Karen Emmons, archivist at the Historic Charleston Foundation, for her help in securing images for this book. Likewise, Heather Gilbert of the Lowcountry Digital Library has been a tremendous help in securing good images for this work. My friend Sarah Fick is a professional historian whose work I admire very much, and she has graciously batted back and forth theories that are reflected in the work that follows. Likewise, Professor Robert Stockton is an expert whose thoughts and previous work I have frequently used.

Lastly, my parents, George and Dorothy Eberle, deserve a special word for instilling in me an interest in all things historical, but especially our built environment. I don't remember a time that I was ever unaware of the importance of preserving historic places and documenting their stories. Whether by nature or nurture, Mom and Dad are responsible for that.

I hope that you enjoy the result.

Introduction

If someone tried to learn Charleston's geography from guidebooks, he or she would be forgiven for thinking that the Crosstown—that gash of 1960s infrastructure that divides the upper and lower peninsula with its six lanes of traffic—was the edge of the world. Tourist maps might as well show mermaids and sea monsters cavorting along the side of the highway for all the tourist traffic that makes its way beyond Highway 17 to points northward on the peninsula.

Locals know better. Locals, to be sure, take advantage of the iconic open spaces like the Waterfront Park at times, but they do not use them for personal recreation as much as one might imagine. After all, how many Parisians visit the Eiffel Tower regularly? Residents of the South's most historic and beautiful city know that the best outdoor public space is actually three miles from the Battery where tour buses and carriages rarely go.

Hampton Park is a different kind of park than anyone would expect in Charleston. Hampton Park is a Charleston park, but it is completely unlike Charleston. Charleston is world famous for its highly manicured gardens with clipped lawns, sculpted shrubs and mathematically precise layouts hidden behind the massive walls and iron gates of neoclassical compounds and Colonial manses. Hampton Park is the opposite of that.

Hampton Park came of age at the turn of the last century. Charleston had largely stayed concentrated on the tip of a peninsula near where the original walled city had been laid out. After two centuries, a person could still easily walk from one side of the city to the other in about an hour. By the first years of the twentieth century, Charleston was finally joining the movement of modern America. It was casting off the economic hardships caused by the Civil War and starting to develop a broad, industrial middle class that had never existed in the South before. New industries like phosphate mining and fertilizer manufacturing were springing up, and Charleston was starting to disconnect from its traditional, agrarian foundation.

Hampton Park was both figuratively and literally a breath of fresh air in Charleston. Its naturalistic character was an antidote to the cramped conditions endured by families living on a lower peninsula densely packed with mansions, tenements and commerce. It was immediately a wildly popular destination for city dwellers who took advantage of new trolley lines and a few private cars to access the "remote" getaway for a few hours. Hampton Park offered, and still offers, wide-open fields of grass, walking trails and overflowing flower beds.

But while Hampton Park is today one of the most popular outdoor destinations for residents, its history is much more complex and fascinating than just that. It says something about Charlestonians that they landscape with oaks that no one who plants will live to enjoy at maturity: Charlestonians have a long view of history and their place in it. They are acutely aware of their past—both good and bad—and take great pains to share it with those who visit. And so, it is important to go back to the very start. The story of Hampton Park actually began more than three hundred years ago and includes early plantation life, Revolutionary War battles, horseracing, the Civil War, industrial development, civic spectacle, professional baseball, a zoo and disco. But before all of that, the story begins with Native Americans.

Chapter 1

NATIVE AMERICANS AND THE PRE-COLONIAL ERA

Kiawah Indians were almost certainly among the first people to use the area that makes up Hampton Park. There is very little physical evidence of pre-colonial use of any portion of the Charleston area and even less of the specific portion that includes Hampton Park. What is definitely known about tribes such as the Kiawah Indians comes from records made by the English settlers of Charleston and modern archaeological studies.

Charleston was established at what is today Charles Towne Landing, a state park, on the west side of the Ashley River. After a stormy crossing of the Atlantic, English colonists arrived in 1670 at a point nearer Beaufort, South Carolina. The settlers encountered initial hostilities with a band of Indians who were possibly in league with the Spanish to the south. The English settlers' early ally and translator, the chief or cassique of the Kiawah tribe, encouraged them to relocate to the "Kyawaw" area instead, only a day's travel northward. Given the risk of living near the Spanish settlements to the south, the settlers accepted the invitation, and in April 1670, they arrived at "Albemarle poynt at Kyawaw." Their new fortified home, named Charles Towne in late 1670 in honor of the King, was almost directly across the Ashley River from the land that would one day become Hampton Park.

There had been, however, a preexisting settlement of Kiawah Indians in the same spot claimed by the English settlers. The tribes were small, with the Kiawah totaling perhaps 160 members in the late seventeenth century.

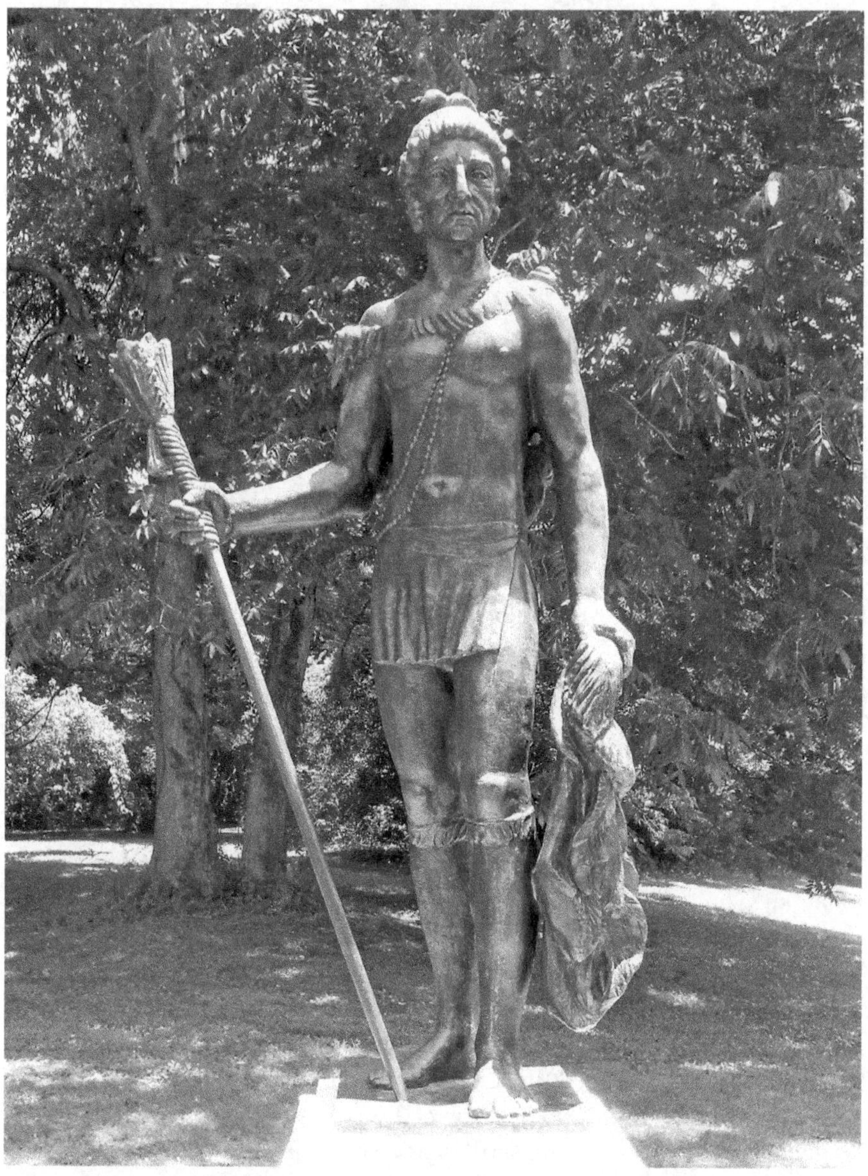

In honor of the Kiawah Indians, who encouraged British settlement along the Ashley River in 1670, a statute of their cassique (chief) was erected at Charles Towne Landing. The sculpture is by Willard Hirsch and was erected in 1971 as part of the tricentennial. *Photo by author.*

Indeed, the entire population of all coastal tribes in South Carolina was about 1,750 before the English arrived. By the time Charles Towne was settled, the number had dropped to about 1,000. Disease, warfare among the tribes, hostilities with the Spanish and tribe relocations cut the number to about 250 total Native Americans remaining in the area by the mid-eighteenth century. By comparison, the first boat of English colonists, the *Carolina*, carried 93 passengers.[1]

Considering the extremely low density of inhabitants, it is not surprising that there are so few footprints of early life along the Ashley River, and the breadth of the native community in the area surrounding Charles Towne Landing is unknown. Making documentation even harder is that the local tribes congregated near one another in loose, coastal communities during the summer, but they broke into smaller bands in the fall and moved inland for the winter. One of the few descriptions of the living patterns of the coastal tribes from the period indicates that they would have been diffuse: "Nor dwell they in Towns, but in straggling Plantations; often removing for the better conveniency of Hunting…"

Nevertheless, evidence of at least some Native American structures have been found at Charles Towne Landing, including post holes for a possible ceremonial building. Nearby sheds, possibly for storing ceremonial items, and platforms for observers have been discovered. Other excavations have revealed shards of pottery perhaps as old as 500 BC.

The tribes are believed to have returned each year to basically the same spots. Given the long history of use of the area and the possibility of at least quasi-permanent structures at the site, it is certain that tribe members were familiar with the opposite side of the Ashley River. Indeed, the topography of the site of Hampton Park would seem to hold obvious advantages for tribes during periods of hostilities with neighboring tribes. Unlike the low-lying land at Albemarle Point, the ground on the northern side of the Ashley River rises surprisingly from the marshes to one of the highest points within at least a mile. Its defensive benefits could not have been missed by those living in the area. Indeed, the rise in elevation was prominent enough to be noted on early maps of Charleston and was, at some unknown later point, known familiarly as "Indian Hill."

Chapter 2
The Colonial Era

A decade after the founding of Charles Towne, the leaders of the nascent city chose to relocate to a better position at the end of a long, narrow peninsula about six and one half miles long between the Ashley and Cooper Rivers. The settlers built a defensive wall around their new home, and development spread quickly, with new homes, stores and churches springing up. Farther up the peninsula, the land narrowed considerably, and the two rivers almost pinched together near present-day Line Street before the land widened again to a distance of about ten miles. The land on which Hampton Park would later be built was so remote by early eighteenth-century standards that it was not even shown on the leading map of the time, drawn by Edward Crisp in 1711.

The upper peninsula was known as the Charles Towne Neck. The Broad Path (now King Street) was laid out along the spine of the peninsula to avoid the settlers' needing to build costly bridges to traverse creeks and marshes. It was not long before agricultural development began taking hold, and King Street became the colony's first major highway.

The first colonists to get grants from the agents of the Lords Proprietors (the eight supporters of King Charles who had been granted the entire colony to run largely as they saw fit) received strips of land stretching from the shore of the Ashley River to the shore of the Cooper River. The parcels were stacked on each other like layers of a cake from Oyster Point at the southern tip of the peninsula upward. The early understanding of the layout of the land was not always accurate, and when surveys came back, they

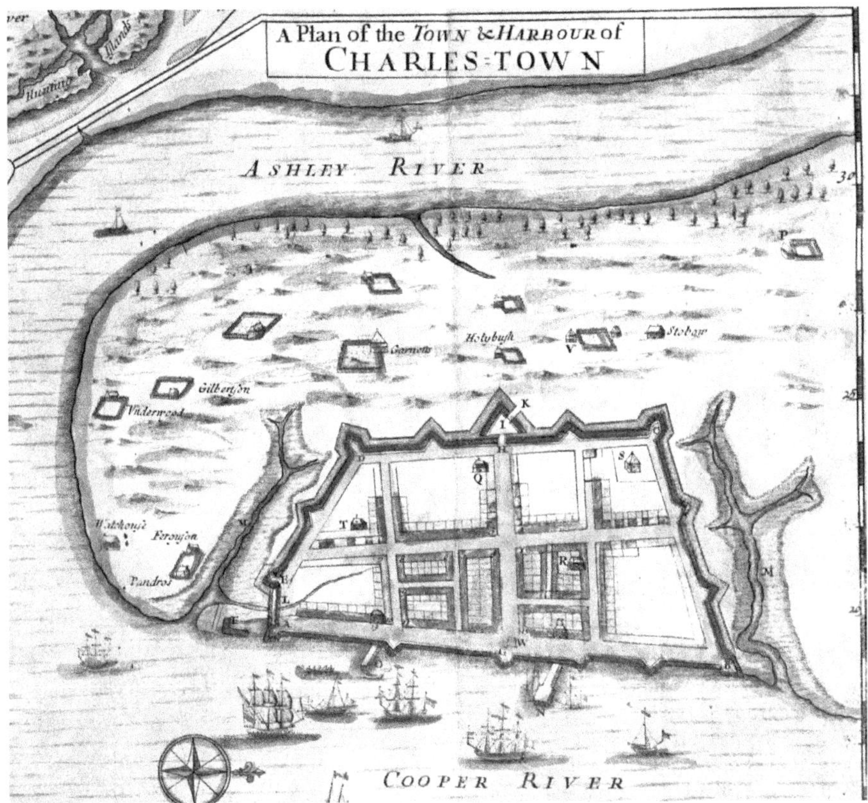

This map was published Edward Crisp in London and shows the eight blocks of the newly relocated Charles Towne at the southern end (left) of the Charleston peninsula. Hampton Park (and the entire upper peninsula) was not included to the right. *Library of Congress.*

often revealed that there simply was not as much land as had been granted. In one of the worst cases of overselling, Joseph Dalton, who had arrived on the very first ship in Charleston, received 1,150 acres or as much land as existed sandwiched between grants to Richard Cole to the south and George Bedon and Hugh Carterett to the north. In the end, the land for Dalton amounted to only 423 acres. Included in those 423 acres is what today makes up Hampton Park.

The chain of title for most of Charleston is incomplete because of lost, destroyed or unfiled records of conveyance. Very early on, Daniel Cartwright had acquired about 190 acres that had been part of the Dalton Grant. His name, or perhaps that of a family member, appears on the 1711 Edward Crisp map of Charleston, and his name appears in the June 21,

In Edward Crisp's broader view of the Charleston peninsula from 1711, the area for Hampton Park was shown well outside the safety of the walled city. The property was marked with the name of its owner until 1738, Daniel Cartwright. *Library of Congress.*

1735 *South Carolina Gazette* as part of the description of another parcel on the Neck. He sold that tract and another section to the north to John Braithwaite on May 8, 1738.[2]

The use of the property in the earliest days of Charleston's history and before has not yet been established. No doubt, English settlers would have been familiar with the existence of what would become Hampton Park. Indian Hill rises sharply from the surrounding land to a point twenty-two feet above sea level (about ten feet above the surrounding land), making it the highest point on the Charleston peninsula. The point is immediately westward of The Citadel mess hall today and enjoys a grand view of the Ashley River.

The high point was popularly thought to have been built as an Indian burial ground, and the myth continued until 1962, when an archaeologist from North Carolina's Brunswick State Historic Site, Stanley A. South, was permitted by The Citadel to dig into Indian Hill in search of its origin. He quickly determined that Indian Hill might have been used by Native Americans, but it was certainly not built by them; it is a naturally occurring rise in the landscape.[3]

The focus of Smith's archaeology shifted instead to the remnants of early buildings at the site. The researchers had located a partly exposed brick and performed a limited excavation. The dig revealed two buildings. The first was a smaller structure with a brick foundation wall. Some Indian pottery shards were located, and the researchers speculated that there must have been interactions between the colonists and the Native Americans. Pieces of

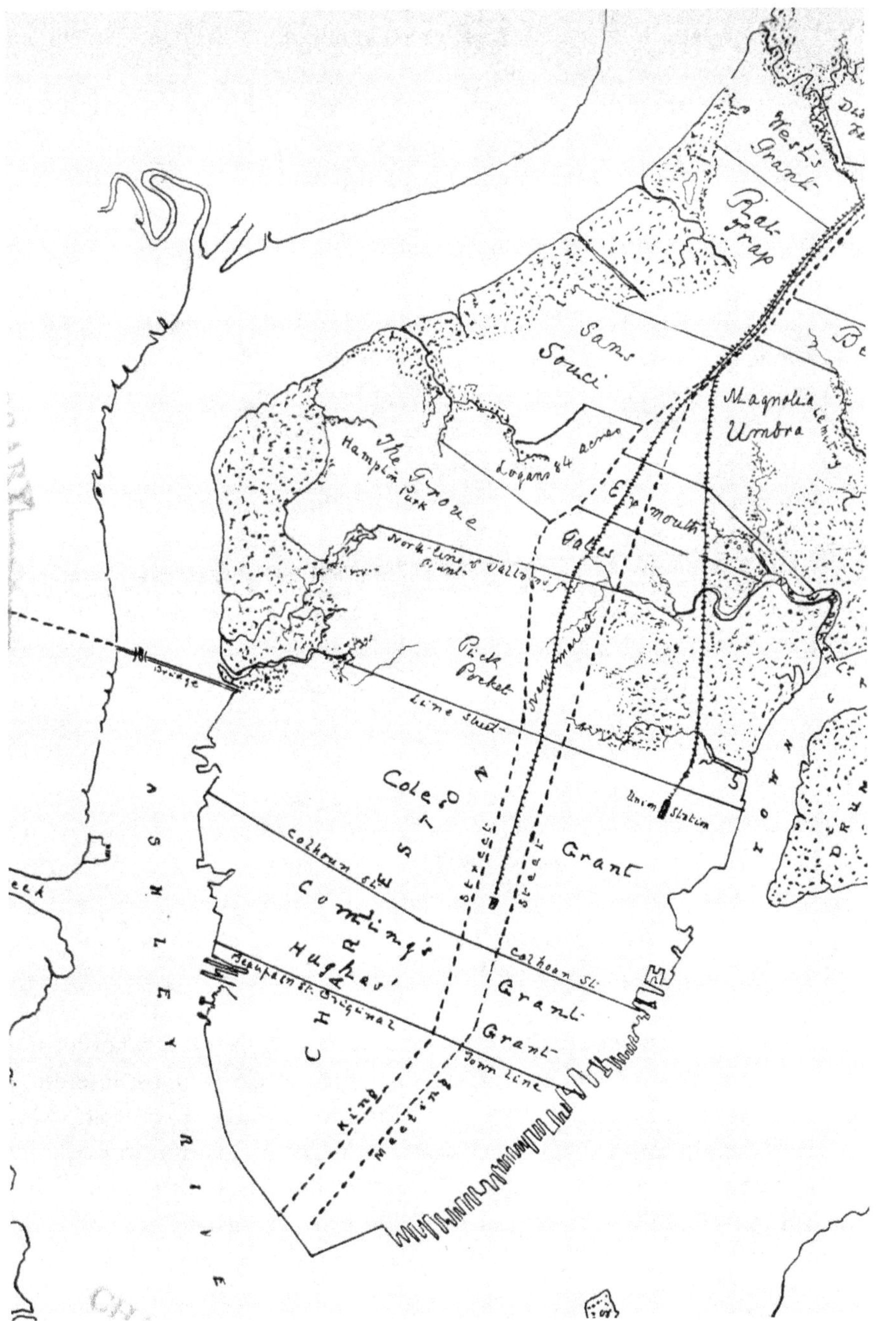

Henry A.M. Smith prepared a map of the earliest land grants for the Charleston peninsula in 1917. Hampton Park was later contructed on a grant to Joseph Dalton, shown on the map by its later name, "The Grove." *Charleston County Library, South Carolina Room.*

the building showed no evidence of burning, and the researchers concluded that the building was likely pulled down.

Nearby, the remains of a larger building were found. The second building was built on a brick and tabby foundation that was approximately 20 feet by 32 feet (640 square feet). It was apparently a dwelling for which the first, smaller building was an outbuilding of unknown purpose. Rubble inside the perimeter of the dwelling showed heavy char marks suggesting that the building had burned down. Artifacts found at the site included a wine bottle, pipes, pottery (both English and Native American), a shutter pintle, a nail and a buckle. Debris established that the house had finished plaster walls and what was perhaps a partially dug out basement. The pipe fragments were dated to about 1689, and the form of the wine bottle and style of the pottery were typical of the period from 1680 to 1720.

Nothing else is known about these early buildings, including which owner built them, whether they were simple or ornate or when they were burned and pulled down. Given the absence of late eighteenth-century artifacts at the site, the house and outbuilding were apparently gone before the mid-eighteenth century. The archaeological research had a very limited scope, and further exploration may reveal more information in the future.

In 1769, the property belonged to John Gibbes (1733–1780), who added a portion of marshlands to his farm that year with a new grant. His property ran north from present-day Congress Street and included what are today Hampton Park, the Hampton Park Terrace neighborhood, The Citadel and much of the Wagener Terrace neighborhood, including Lowndes Grove plantation. Possibly because of the addition of the marshlands the previous year, Gibbes had his property surveyed in May 1770. By that time, his land totaled 232 acres and was known as Orange Grove or, more commonly, Grove Plantation.

A copy of the original plat survives, but how closely the finer details of the original were copied is unknown. The surveyor was clearly most interested in the metes and bounds of Gibbes' land, and specific trees were noted with distances measured between them along the property lines. The topography of the land itself and any landmarks are totally absent from the plat, save one feature. The surveyor noted a gate to the property near King Street and a long, straight road leading to the front of a house. The image on the 1770 plat is the only known drawing of the house at Orange Grove.

It does not appear that there is a connection between Gibbes's plantation and the earlier buildings discovered during the 1962 archaeological investigation; in maps and plats, Orange Grove's house was consistently

John Gibbes' plantation was surveyed in 1770. The plat survives in a later copy prepared for the city. It is unknown whether the original surveyor intended his drawing to represent actual features and whether the copyist's version carefully reproduced them. Nevertheless, for now, it includes the only known image of the house at Orange Grove Plantation. *Charleston County Library, South Carolina Room.*

shown at least several hundred feet northeast of Indian Hill approximately in front of Summerall Chapel at The Citadel.

Whether the copy of the surveyor's drawing was meant to represent the actual house cannot be determined until another image of the house is found. The house shown might have simply been a generic icon to designate its existence. The inclusion of the drawing on the 1770 plat, however, is curious for its detail. Unlike later map makers, who marked the house at Grove Plantation with a simple rectangle, the surveyor in 1770 actually drew a distinct house's front. The image is ambiguous, but it shows a simple, symmetrical façade with matching chimneys with flared tops at either end. What seems to represent a one-story, full-length porch is shown on the front of the house; others have interpreted the horizontal block as a crude effort to show a second floor. The roof form is not at all clear and might be the surveyor's effort to document either a hipped, gable roof or Dutch roof.

Chapter 3
The Revolutionary War

The lead-up to the American Revolutionary War is well known to all schoolchildren. Following a long period of increasingly difficult relations between the colonies and England, the colonists' patience ended in 1775 with the Battles of Lexington and Concord, and the Declaration of Independence was signed on July 4, 1776. Less well known is that the first decisive victory of the colonies had actually occurred about one week earlier near Charleston, South Carolina. British major general Henry Clinton and Admiral Peter Parker had joined forces just north of the city and planned to take the yet-unfinished Fort Moultrie on Sullivan's Island. The colonial forces dug in and repelled both the land and naval forces, and the British were forced to retreat. The British returned their attention to New York and New England and did not attempt another inroad in the South for more than one year. But Major General Clinton would be back.

Following a long period without any significant victories, the British took Savannah, Georgia, on December 29, 1778, and established a foothold in the South. As soon as the city was under firm control of the British, attention turned to Charleston. Major General Clinton left New York in December 1779 to personally oversee the campaign against the South's crown jewel, the city that had handed him such a humiliating loss in June 1776. On February 11, 1780, a fleet of almost fifty ships arrived on the South Carolina coast, and the troops began their progress toward Charleston from John's Island with almost no resistance. The British established themselves at Fort Johnson on James Island and began making plans to move on Charleston.

The British forces massed at Lining's Point near the original settlement of Charles Towne. Directly across the river was Grove Plantation. Along the Ashley River at that point, the Charleston peninsula is set far back from navigable water, and wide marshes extend into the river, shielding the land by hundreds of feet at places. Grove Plantation, however, occupied an enviable position on high ground. As best can be determined from plats and maps, the main house was located about where The Citadel's Parade Grounds are today. About one-quarter mile northwest was a point of strategic advantage where the marshes receded and exposed a point of high land. Today, the spit of land is near the western end of St. Margaret Street. In the late eighteenth century, it was the first spot north of Charleston at which a ferry from across the river could land, and it was known as Gibbes' Landing.

Meanwhile, by March 28, 1780, the British had sent troops as far upriver as either Bee's Ferry or perhaps Drayton Hall, had crossed over the Ashley River and had begun their march to Charleston down the spine of the peninsula. The British arrived at the neck of Charleston within two days.

On March 30, 1780, General William Moultrie, the hero of the Battle of Sullivan's Island, reported minor skirmishes with the British near Gibbes' property. One Hessian jager captain named Johann Ewald wrote of his experiences with the British forces. On the evening of March 30, 1780, the jagers were posted at Grove Plantation, where he "did picket duty in one of the most beautiful pleasure gardens of the world." The next day, Captain Ewald and other men were ordered to advance "through the wood in front of Gibbes' house and through the swamp on the left bank of the Ashley River, so that the General's staff could reconnoiter. I pushed my party without mishap as far as the dams across Black Creek, which are within range of the enemy's cannon, and was honored with three shots. The picket was posted in the wood close to Gibbes' Negro houses." According to Captain Ewald, "The county around Gibbes' house has been made a park and depot for the siege, and the greenhouse a laboratory." There was damage done: "Major Moncrieff of the Engineers had all the wooden houses in the neighborhood torn down today. From the boards and beams of these he had his men make mantelets to be used in building the inner side of the batteries and redoubts and also the cheeks of the embrasures." Nowhere in the detailed journal did Captain Ewald note that Grove Plantation had been destroyed.[4]

Major General Clinton, who must have relished his advances against General Moultrie, arrived with large numbers of troops who set up camp near Grove Street. Their position spread from Gibbes' Landing on one side

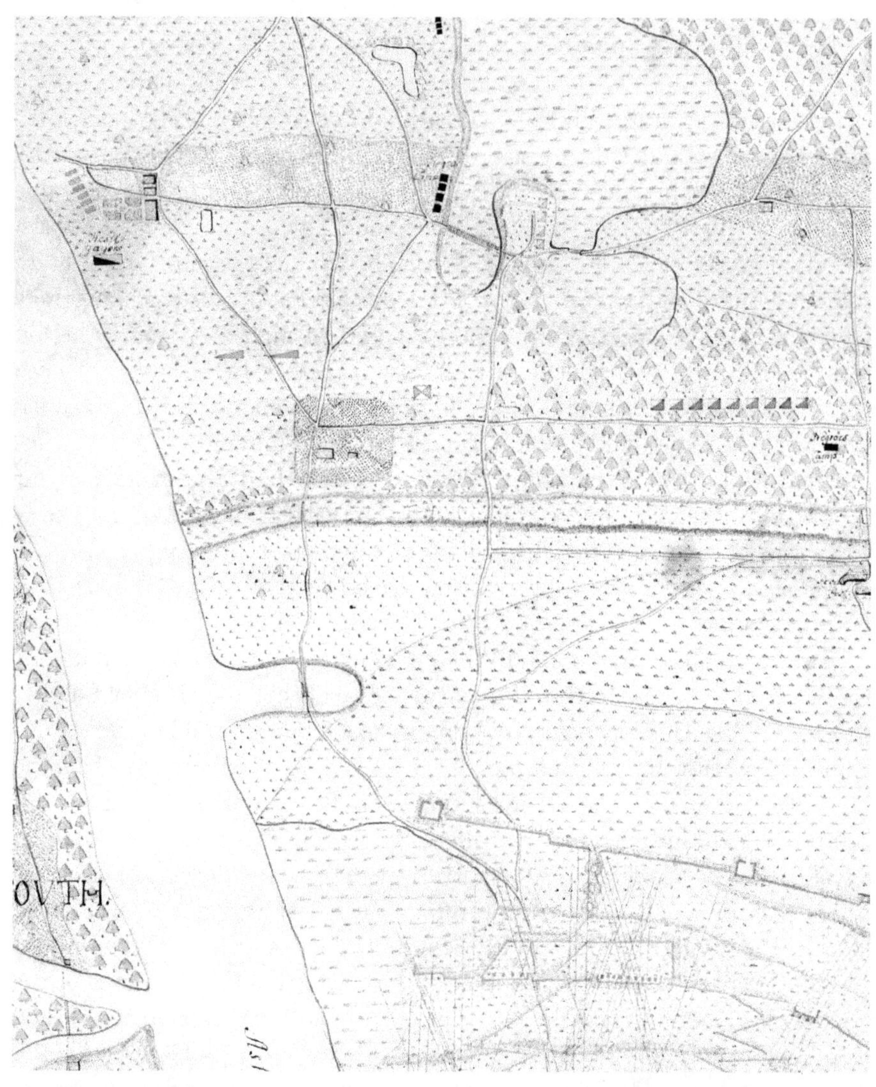

A map drawn in 1780 by British forces shows the location of Hessian soldiers stationed adjacent to Orange Grove Plantation. Although the buildings (shown at upper left) have no special details, the map is notable for confirming formal, geometric gardens at the site. *Library of Congress.*

This engraving, known as *The Siege of Charleston*, represents events of 1780. Although the relative position of the British troops on the upper peninsula near Orange Grove is correct, the topography—with rolling hills—is purely imagined. *New York Public Library.*

of the peninsula to New Market Creek on the other, completely cutting off Charleston from any supply lines. British forces remaining at Lining's Point began ferrying supplies across the Ashley River and disembarked at Gibbes' Landing.

Grove Plantation's role as the staging area for the artillery was a more significant role for Hampton Park's land than one might expect. The Siege of Charleston was just that—a siege and not a battle. The competing forces picked at individual soldiers, but mainly the "fighting" was limited to an unrelenting storm of cannon shot from each stronghold. Of course, the British enjoyed the advantage of free movement and replenished materials while Charleston was surrounded.

Eventually, the Colonials decided to surrender, but General Clinton refused the terms offered by General Moultrie each time. The constant barrage of British fire took its toll. According to General Moultrie:

The fire was incessant almost the whole night; cannon balls whizzing and shells hissing continually amongst us; ammunition chests and temporary magazines blowing up; great guns bursting and wounded men groaning along the lines. It was a dreadful night. It was our last great effort, but it availed us nothing. After this our military ardor was much abated; we began to cool, and we cooled gradually, and on the 11th of May we capitulated, and on the morning of the 12th we marched out and gave up the town.

When the British learned that there were only about 1,500 healthy colonial soldiers, they complimented the colonials on their gallant defense. In all, the British lost only 76 men in taking the South's most important city.[5]

Grove Plantation did not fare well during the conflict. By the outbreak of the Siege of Charleston, it already had well-established and extensive gardens. In 1822, Alexander Garden, the son of the like-named botanist, wrote a series of reminiscences about the American Revolution in which he heavily romanticized stories of colonial leaders while serving up screeds against the British. His two books might be considered very broad guidelines to history, but their accuracy is doubtful on the details. For example, Garden's works often contain detailed transcriptions of conversations from fifty years earlier to which he was not a party with no sources mentioned.

One particular account, though, perhaps has at least a hint of truth to it. Garden's wife, Mary Anna Gibbes, was the niece of John Gibbes of Grove Plantation. According to one anecdote from Garden, Gibbes was away from Orange Grove visiting his brother, Robert Gibbes, when the British crossed the Ashley River in March 1780 and landed near his plantation. At the time, Orange Grove had been "improved not only with taste in the disposition of the grounds, but by the introduction of numberless exotics of the highest beauty. [John Gibbes] had, in addition, a green-house and pinery, in the best condition."[6] (A "pinery" is a mainly British term for a building, perhaps a hothouse, in which pineapples are grown.)

A British major named Sheridan arrived at the home of Robert Gibbes and was asked whether General Clinton's forces had taken the city yet. Not knowing that he was in the presence of John Gibbes, Sheridan responded, "I fear not, but we have made glorious havoc of the property in the vicinity." Sheridan went on, "I yesterday witnessed the destruction of an elegant establishment belonging to an arch Rebel, who luckily for himself was absent. You would have been delighted to see how quickly the pine apples [*sic*] were shared among our men, and how rapidly his trees and ornamental shrubs were leveled with the dust." To that unintended attack,

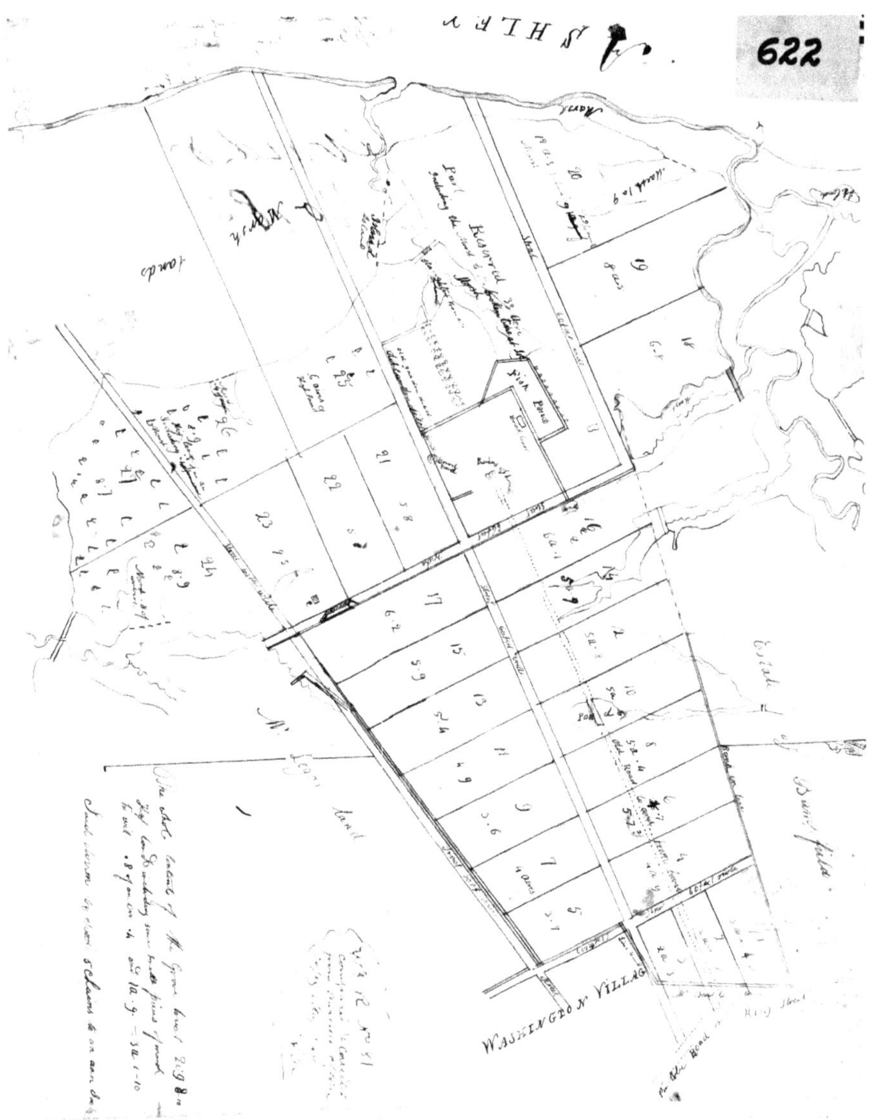

Following the Revolutionary War, Orange Grove Plantation was subdivided and sold off. When this plat was drawn, remnants of formal landscaping were still extant, along with a few other fragments of the Gibbes plantation, such as the "ruins" of the main house. The Ashley River to the west is shown at the top of the map. *Charleston County Register of Mesne Conveyances.*

John Gibbes, who recognized the description of his plantation, responded, "I hope that the Almighty will cause the arm of the scoundrel who struck the first blow to wither to his shoulder." Such a mild exchange would pass without comment today, but the donnybrook had so upset Gibbes that he retired to his bed and died.

There are no other reports of the British wantonly destroying houses they commandeered in their march on Charleston, and it is difficult to imagine a reason for purposefully destroying a useable house while occupying the surrounding land. If Garden's timing is correct, a more likely (but also unconfirmed) theory would be that the house was accidentally destroyed or was the victim of colonial bombardment of the British position during the forty-two-day siege.

While Garden's version of events might have been embellished for romantic impact, there is no doubt that John Gibbes died in 1780. In 1794, Robert Gibbes was the executor of his brother's estate and placed an advertisement in the newspaper calling for all persons with claims against his brother's estate to come forward so the estate could be closed: "It is hoped that the above will be seriously attended to, and that those concerned will not esteem it unreasonable, when they reflect that they have already had fourteen years to make up their payment."[7]

John Gibbes had no children, and Grove Plantation was divided up for sale. By April 1786, the plantation had been divided into twenty-seven lots ranging from three to twelve acres that were listed for sale in the newspaper.[8] The site of the plantation house and gardens was reserved, but the remainder of the property was probably meant for small farms. One exception was the sale of several of the parcels along the northern edge of the tract; those parcels were joined, and a new plantation house, known as Lowndes Grove, was built on them around 1800. During the same period, the old farm was already getting use as a pleasure ground for visitors; in 1786, the German Fusiliers gave a "very genteel" entertainment to their membership at the "seat of the late John Gibbes" that included dinner, a display of the troops and thirteen rounds of toasts to all manner of honorees.[9]

None of the listings for the various sales referred to any house on the grounds, and a plat from 1787 shows what was called "Ruins of house" with the tree-lined avenue behind the house still intact. Also shown was a "brick house" of unknown purpose slightly to the northwest of the ruins; the brick dwelling remained until the 1830s at least, but it was elsewhere shown as having been burned by the early twentieth century.[10] The end of the inlet had been dammed to create a "Fish Pond." Those lots directly in front of the plantation ruins would be assembled into what is today Hampton Park. On one of the lots, a low-lying area, perhaps a tidal creek, is shown where, more than a century later, the Sunken Gardens would be built.

At least a large portion of the lots went unclaimed, and on February 4, 1790, an advertisement appeared in the *City Gazette and Daily Advertiser* announcing the sale of "that beautiful spot," Grove Plantation, at public sale. Another advertisement ran in August 1790 that seems to have referred to the subdivided parcels being available for sale: "A Number of valuable lots on that beautiful farm known by the name the GROVE, late the property of John Gibbes, Esq; deceased, which will be laid out in the quantity of acres which may suit the purchasers. Many of them will be within sixty feet of the new race course, intended to be laid out next week, and will afford an uninterrupted view of the spectators of that manly amusement."[11]

Chapter 4
THE WASHINGTON RACE COURSE

For almost a century after the Gibbeses' use of Hampton Park for part of their Orange Grove Plantation ended, the aristocratic use of the land continued. From 1792 until the Civil War, the Washington Race Course, a one-mile loop around today's Hampton Park, featured the finest horse racing in the South.[12]

Charleston had a long history of horse racing. The first horse race in Charleston occurred in 1734 at a temporary course near a public house with a saddle and bridle worth twenty pounds as the prize. By 1735, the York Course was the first permanent track in Charleston, and races were held each year, normally with a prize of a silver trophy worth about £100. In 1754, a subscription was organized to fund the construction of a new racecourse nearer town, and the New Market Race Course was first used on February 19, 1760. The New Market Race Course was between Line and Huger Streets, bounded by King and Meeting Streets. Wealthy planters raised, traded, bought and even imported Thoroughbreds that were raced both in Charleston and at other places in the Southeast.

When the Revolution began, attention turned away from racing. Some horses were used in the colonial military effort as chargers; others were hidden in the swamps near their owners' plantations to safeguard them from seizure by the British. When the Revolutionary War ended in 1783, the Lowcountry was eager to resume its old ways. Indeed, the local interest in the sport of kings had even grown. The historian of the South Carolina Jockey Club said this: "The war being over, and peace being duly declared, not only a new era for politics commenced, and a new method of thinking had arisen, but a *new* and more vigorous impulse was given to the sports of the Turf."

In August 1791, twenty members of Charleston's elite combined to purchase a portion of Orange Grove Plantation from Robert Gibbes (the brother of John Gibbes) as a new venue for horse racing. The new Washington Race Course was opened, and the old course was vacated at New Market. Members of the initial group included William Alston, William Washington, Andrew Johnson, Wade Hampton (the father of Civil War general and governor Wade Hampton) and other horse breeders. The first Race Week at the new Washington Race Course was held on February 15, 1792, at the new course and was won by Fox Hunter, owned by Lynch. The main event was the Jockey Club Purse, a race of four heats. Washington Race Course was a one-mile sandy oval course, which was basically the size and shape of Mary Murray Boulevard, the boulevard circling Hampton Park.

By 1829, some members of the original group wanted to sell the racecourse, but others were concerned about the validity of any sale. After nearly forty years, many of the original twenty owners of the racecourse had died, and it was not clear just who owned shares in the venture. On May 15, 1829, one of the members, James E. McPherson, filed a lawsuit over the issue. He asked the court to order a notice of publication of the suit asking anyone with a claim to the property to come forward. The court ordered the land sold, with the proceeds to be divided among those the court had determined owned an interest.

The South Carolina Jockey Club had been formed on December 20, 1826, and, at the suggestion of member John Lyde Wilson, it decided to pursue a permanent home for its races when the Washington Race Course came up for sale. On June 6, 1836, the nearly sixty-four acres were offered at a public sale and bought by the South Carolina Jockey Club for $5,000.

After taking over the course, the South Carolina Jockey Club undertook several improvements. Originally, the starting posts for the Washington Race Course were located near the southeast turn of the oval course. On July 8, 1829, Felicite Godet died, and her property on the Neck of Charleston was sold by the sheriff on January 4, 1831. Her land, which today is at the southwest corner of Ashley Avenue and Moultrie Street, was described in the deed as "near the Race ground directly opposite the starting post." The basic layout of the course was shifted following a meeting on February 27, 1837, and the starting post was moved to the opposite side of the course at the northwest turn. At the same time, the club realized that the course

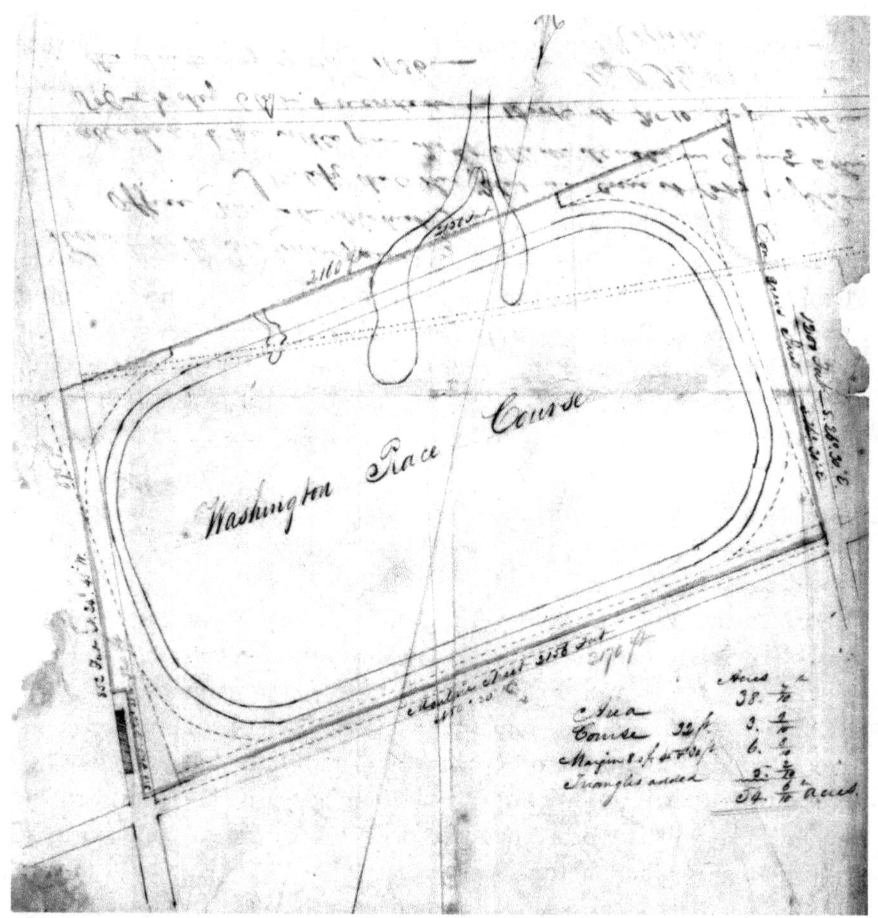

The Washington Race Course was already over forty years old when a plat was drawn of the land in anticipation of its sale to the South Carolina Jockey Club in 1836. *Charleston County Register of Mesne Conveyances.*

had always been forty feet short of a mile, and the mistake was corrected. Two "gentlemen of scientific attainment," Major Parker and R.Q. Pinckney, prepared a diagram of the newly improved course.

Also in 1837, a new grandstand was erected near the starting post for the comfort of ladies and invited guests of the Jockey Club. The architect for the new stands was Charles Reichardt, a German architect, whose most famous project was the Charleston Hotel on Meeting Street. When ladies arrived at the racecourse in their carriages, they would pull to a rear entrance, enter through a covered archway and climb a flight of stairs to a grand

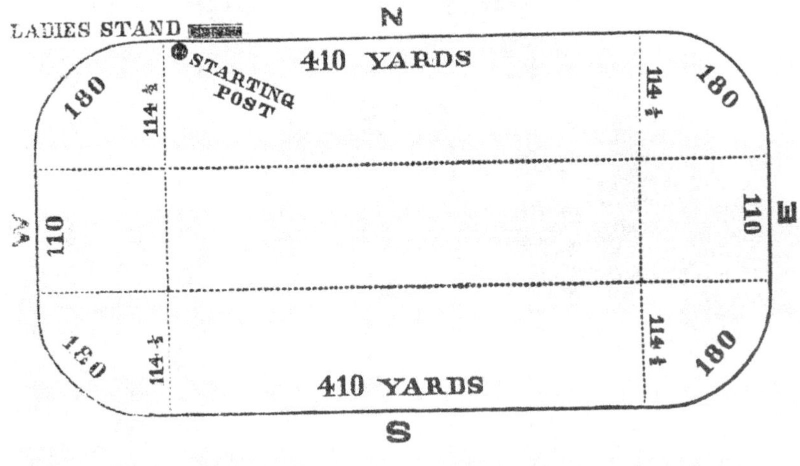

The track at the Washington Race Course had never been precisely one mile long. Upon purchasing the track, the Jockey Club resurveyed the land and fixed its configuration. *Reproduced for a report by the Jockey Club.*

saloon. The viewing room provided views of the course through floor-to-ceiling windows and had a wide balcony capable of holding several hundred spectators. Smaller rooms for refreshments were located at either end of the main viewing hall. The whole building was carpeted and "furnished in good taste, and reserved for ladies that may honor the Club with their attendance." Beneath the viewing rooms, on the ground floor, were rooms for the jockeys and stewards for weighing and changing clothes. A separate stand was built next to the Ladies' Stands and was used by the club's officers and the timers of the races. A stout picket fence was placed around the viewing stands and for some distance around the track to keep the public out while not interfering with the view of the course.

While the main facilities at the Washington Race Course were for the comfort of the members, "respectable strangers from abroad, or from other States" were invited to enjoy the benefits of the course. They were not permitted to pay any admission for the enjoyments of the racecourse.

H. Bosse was hired to create this engraving of the new grandstands by the South Carolina Jockey Club from a daguerreotype by D.L. Glenn. His work illustrated an 1857 history of the club.

The grandstands at the racecourse were originally somewhat plain in the 1830s. By the time the only known photograph of them was taken in 1865, they had been modified considerably. Still, the two segments of the original structure could be readily identified. *Library of Congress.*

Instead, upon arriving, they were treated as guests of the club and given tickets for the events, and a ribbon entitled them to the benefits of the club during their stays.

Originally, the entire course had been open to public view, but member John Wilson suggested enclosing the course with a fence so that the club could charge admission to the events. In 1842, the club spent $1,200 to have R.Q. Pinckney build a 6,448-foot-long fence around the racecourse. Still, the public could attend the races for a charge, but once on the grounds, there were many distractions. For those interested in watching the races, there was a Citizens' Stand, another suggestion by Wilson, which was open to the public at large at no cost, with two levels. The Citizens' Stand was built by George Cramer at his own expense starting in late 1835. The building was 200 feet long and 25 feet wide to accommodate one thousand viewers. As part of his deal with the Jockey Club, Cramer was given the right to rent the ground-floor rooms for $200 a year and use them as he saw fit. On the first floor, Cramer built a series of reception rooms, which were "fitted up in good taste" and which the public could used for either small or large parties. On the second floor were rows of seats to watch the races.

During Race Week, a festival atmosphere took over all around the grounds. Various booths provided food, "fun and frolic." The vendors catered to those who "require, in a long day, to have their inner man regaled from time to time." On an adjoining farm that the club purchased, the club rented out stables to those who had traveled to Charleston from out of state with horses.

In 1854, artist Charles Fraser described the atmosphere that overtook the city during Race Week:

> *Schools were dismissed. The judges, not unwillingly, adjourned the Courts, for they were deserted by lawyers, suitors and witnesses. Clergymen thought it no impropriety to see a well contested race; and if grave physicians played truant, they were sure to be found in the crowd at the race ground...The whole week was devoted to pleasure and the interchanges of conviviality; nor were the ladies unnoticed, for the Race ball, given to them by the Jockey Club, was always the most splendid of the season.*[13]

Races at American courses were generally held twice each year; in Charleston, the most important horse racing occurred only in February. The historian of the club wrote about this unusual choice: "The question has often been asked, why does not the South Carolina Jockey Club, with its ample means, have *two* meetings a year, instead of one?" His response? "Our pleasures have a higher relish when they are rarely used. The keenest sense of delight is sure to be blunted by a too frequent repetition."[14]

Especially since the course was used for horse racing only one week a year, the vast majority of the time, the racecourse was not in use. So what was the land used for when no races were taking place? Dueling, for one.

Whether attracted by its level, open ground or perhaps its remote location, the Washington Race Course and the nearby fields were a popular choice for fights of honor by the early nineteenth century. The earliest known duel involved John McPherson and an unknown Motte in 1806.[15]

Not uncommonly, the source of the disagreement began during political debate. For example, on September 29, 1812, William Bay, the son of a local judge, was shot and killed in a duel with William Crafts. Their disagreement was a "mere trifle," with Crafts saying that the local bishop was "too much a Gentleman & a man of sense" to be a Republican. Bay, a Republican himself, took issue, and the matter escalated. A physical fight broke out when Crafts described a politician as "another tall, awkward, gawky, Yankee looking fellow as Bay." Crafts requested a duel, but Bay declined. After some pressure, Bay changed his mind, and he and Crafts went out "to or near the Race course," where Bay was shot in the heart and died immediately "without uttering a groan."[16] Later, some witnesses claimed that Crafts had shot before the word was given, but others charitably agreed his gun had misfired by accident.

In 1856 alone, the property hosted two duels. The first involved Colonel John Cunningham and L.M. Hatch, the editor of the *Standard*. On July 21, 1856, an editorial by Colonel Cunningham ran in the *Evening News*, which drew a response from the *Standard*. Each paper returned volley on the next two days before the dispute moved from the editorial pages to the personal correspondence of the gentlemen.

Colonel Cunningham wrote to the *Standard* demanding to know who had written the response to his own editorial, and Hatch stated that he had. Colonel Cunningham followed up with a charge that Hatch had included "studied and wanton personal insult" and demanded a retraction. Hatch declined, claiming Colonel Cunningham's original editorial in the *Evening News* had started the dispute. More charges and countercharges followed.

Eventually, Colonel Cunningham demanded "the satisfaction due to me" and appointed his friend William Taber to negotiate the details of a duel. Hatch accepted and appointed Samuel Lord as his own representative. The proxies met to hammer out the details, but they were themselves bogged down in disagreement; they could not decide whether the duelists would start with their guns pointed downward (the "rise shot" favored by Lord) or pointed up (the "drop shot" favored by Taber). The representatives brought in two more gentlemen, Alfred Rhett and James Conner, who then selected an umpire named Clarence Cochran. Cochran picked the "rising shot" option, and—finally—the terms were set (although Rhett disagreed with that choice and took the time to write out a dissenting opinion).

On the afternoon of July 28, 1856, Colonel Cunningham and Hatch finally met to settle matters. They traded shots with no injury to either man, and their seconds tried to negotiate a settlement again. Cunningham's representative repeated his demand for a retraction, but Hatch's designee refused. Instead, after what seems like days of needless quibbling, Hatch offered the following: "Mr. Hatch reiterates that his article was responsive to Col. Cunningham's article...which he considered personally insulting...If Col. Cunningham will disclaim any intention personally to insult Mr. Hatch by that article, Mr. Hatch...consents to the withdrawal of both articles."[17] Colonel Cunningham did agree that he meant nothing personal, and with that, the affair concluded.

Later that summer, the political climate of Charleston remained heated. The *Charleston Mercury* was a right-wing weekly newspaper with a decidedly anti-Union leaning. In late September 1856, the newspaper ran a series of three "articles" written by Edmund Rhett, a critic of United States district court judge Magrath who had decided to run for a congressional seat. Not surprisingly, the *Mercury* opposed Judge Magrath as a federal agent who was refusing to do the honorable thing and resign his position to pursue state office, as the paper viewed a state delegate to Congress.

When Edward Magrath, the judge's brother, read the attacks, he was furious and had a letter hand-delivered to the editors of the *Mercury*: "You have... published and circulated insulting and libelous attacks upon my brother, Judge Magrath. To this effect, you have put aside the habitual propriety of a Charleston newspaper, and disregarding the taste and sentiment of the community, have emulated the corruption and licentiousness of a venal press elsewhere."

William Taber, on behalf of his newspaper, took the charges as an attack not just against himself but also against a free press. A duel was set, and the men met at "the usual place," near the Washington Race Course.[18] The principals shot at each other without effect, and their seconds unsuccessfully tried to broker a compromise. A second volley was exchanged, again without injury, and another effort was made to resolve the dispute. Colonel Cunningham, who was returning the favor and acting as Taber's second for the duel, suggested that each side disavow any intent to insult the other. Magrath's representative agreed so long as the following language was added: "That Mr. Taber regrets the publication…of whatever in those articles is personal" and that "Mr. Magrath regrets any thing in the cartel that is offensive." How that addendum differed from the original proposal is far from clear, but it was unacceptable to Taber. Whatever extra meaning Taber might have seen in the final offer proved his undoing. A third round of shots was traded, and Taber was struck in the head, collapsed and died.[19]

Chapter 5

THE CIVIL WAR AND AMERICA'S FIRST MEMORIAL DAY

Charleston will forever be linked with the opening salvos of the United States Civil War. On April 12, 1861, hostilities began when Confederate forces attacked a Federal military installation, Fort Sumter, on a small island in Charleston Harbor. The use of the Washington Race Course for racing was halted during the Civil War. Not only were the planters and wealthy merchants occupied with the hostilities, but they were also safeguarding their horses. Union soldiers commandeered both workaday stock and valuable racing breeds, so owners removed their prize horses to swamps near their country homes to hide them.

During the war, the Washington Race Course was used as a camp for the Rebel forces stationed in Charleston. The camp's greatest strength was its distance inland. Northern guns near the harbor were generally unable to launch shells as far north as the racecourse, so it made for a relatively safe campground. Still, the camp was not free from the violence of war. In the summer of 1862, one particularly gruesome scene played out at the camp. A Confederate deserter was taken to the racecourse in a wagon and made to kneel before an open coffin. Twelve soldiers were lined up to execute him. At the call of "Aim!" the condemned man tore open his shirt to expose his chest; the executioners shot him, and his dead body fell into his coffin to be carried off.[20]

Midway through the war, the belligerents ended prisoner exchanges. Thousands of combatants had to be housed, and housing and care for the Northern soldiers was not a priority. In 1863, prisoners were relocated from

Andersonville, the infamous Georgia prison, to other locations in the South, including Charleston, Savannah and Florence, in advance of Sherman's troops. Some officers were treated better than the enlisted men, but hundreds of Northern troops were simply marched to the old Washington Race Course for warehousing.

The racecourse provided a large, open area far enough up the peninsula to be safe from bombardment, but it had no amenities at all, including tents. The only shade provided was what the prisoners could manage to fashion from their own clothing and blankets. About five thousand Union soldiers were kept at the racecourse. The conditions were so severe that no physical barriers were even needed to restrain the prisoners, and Southern guards simply established a perimeter and marked it with bonfires. Anyone crossing the "dead line" would be shot. Water was hauled to the camp, but only just enough for basic needs; the prisoners even tried digging for water. The holes were as much as ten feet deep and produced brackish water.[21] The prisoners did receive food (which they had to cook themselves), and sympathetic Charlestonians would sometimes risk throwing bread to the prisoners while the guards were not looking.[22] As one prisoner later recalled the scene, "The food thus thrown in was, however, but a drop in that Maelstrom of human miserables, who, actuated by hunger, struggled madly among each other for its possession."[23] Despite having better medical care than in Andersonville, 257 Union soldiers died from exposure, hunger, sickness or some combination during 1864 and early 1865.

When Charleston fell, freed slaves returned to the city by the thousands. Northern newspaper reporter James Redpath came to Charleston, where he assumed responsibility for the school system. He expressed a special concern for the graves of the Union soldiers who had been buried at the Washington Race Course.[24] A committee of citizens formed to build a fence to protect the unmarked graves from horse and foot traffic. A circular was delivered to sympathetic whites and throughout the black community. It read:

Memorial to the Loyal People of South Carolina

> *It is an established fact that a large number of our soldiers died…on what is called the Race Course, in the city of Charleston. It therefore behooves us as a loyal people that a fitting testimonial be made to the memory of those brave men who…were buried…with nothing to mark their last resting-place or to protect their remains. A Committee has been formed to raise a fund to erect a suitable Monument and a Fence to protect it, in honor*

The location of the Union cemetery at the Washington Race Course cannot be pinpointed, but it was near the grandstands at the track's northwest turn. In this photograph, the unidentified building in the distance may be the surviving brick dwelling shown on the plat of Orange Grove Plantation. *Library of Congress.*

> *of those brave soldiers who died in defense of their country, and we do hereby call upon every loyal man, woman and child in the State of South Carolina to aid us in the work, and respectfully ask Minister*[s] *and their Congregations to form committees to raise funds. The contributions have been limited to ten cents each, so that it will give everyone the privilege and debar none from aiding this noble work. South Carolina alone should do the work, and raise ten thousand dollars to complete it, and show the world that…her children have not forgotten the duty they owe to the defenders of our starry flag.*

In response to the circular, a call for volunteers was made at a meeting at the Zion Church on Calhoun Street. Redpath's wife, Mary, urged the members of the church to bring flowers to pile on the "blood-soaked ground." She asked that more and more flowers be brought: "Cover the ground until nothing can be seen but flowers!"

In late April 1865, about two dozen men from the local African Methodist Episcopal churches who called themselves "Friends of the Martyrs" and the "Patriotic Association of Colored Men" built the enclosure for the burial ground. The enclosure was a white picket fence with an arch on which was written, "The Martyrs of the Race Course."[25] The cemetery was located behind the viewing stand at the old racetrack. The precise location is impossible to pinpoint, but it would likely have been slightly northwest of the intersection of Tenth Avenue and Mary Murray Boulevard.

The work on the fence progressed, and a dedication ceremony was set for May 1, 1865. Thousands of African Americans flooded into the city from the surrounding country in colorful dress and streamed toward the old racecourse. Mrs. Redpath rode with General Hatch in his carriage to the ceremony and reported that, along the way, a group of men stopped the carriage, removed the horses and picked up the pole and powered the carriage to the racetrack themselves in gratitude for General Hatch.

The *Charleston News & Courier* described the "immense gathering yesterday. Fully ten thousand persons were present, mostly of the colored population."[26] The exercises on the ground commenced with reading a Psalm, singing a hymn and prayer. The people assembled in the morning and marched to the graves, "nearly every one present bearing a handsome bouquet of flowers. The colored children, about twenty-eight hundred in number, marched first over the burial ground, strewing the graves with their flowers as they passed."

After the children, other civic groups processed, including the "Patriotic Association of Colored Men," an association formed for the purpose of assisting in the distribution of the freedmen's supplies, and the "Mutual Aid Society," an association formed to help bury poor African Americans. After the organized groups, the mass of people approached the graves and laid flowers on them. Meanwhile, the children were singing patriotic songs such as "The Star-Spangled Banner," "America," "Rally Round the Flag" and "John Brown's Body." According to the news report, "The graves at the close of the procession had all the appearance of a mass of roses."

During the exercises, General Hartwell's brigade, consisting of the famous Fifty-fourth Massachusetts, appeared. They marched four abreast around the graves and afterward went through all the evolutions of the manual. Religious and political leaders gave more than thirty speeches while attendees enjoyed picnic lunches and refreshments. The event lasted the entire day, and toward dusk, the crowds dispersed.

Rear Admiral J.A. Dahlgren could not attend, but his letter was read, which made clear the purpose of the festivities: "The object must have the best wishes of every lover of his country. We should never forget the gallant men who have laid down their lives for a great cause, but always keep their memory green." Although other cities assert theirs were the first celebrations of Memorial Day, the events in Charleston on May 1, 1865, establish as strong a claim as any to the rightful honor.

The pageantry surrounding the first Memorial Day ceremony in America was far more elaborate than the simple cemetery for Union soldiers itself. As shown in this rendering from *Harper's Weekly*, by 1867, the spot was starting to suffer from neglect, and the bodies were removed to formal cemeteries soon after. Harper's Weekly, *May 18, 1867.*

By 1867, the graveyard showed signs of neglect. According to a reporter for *Harper's Weekly*, there was a "rude desk" at the grave site that was used for readings during ceremonies. Otherwise, "a mass of tangled grass and herbage nearly hides from sight the little head boards which mark the graves."[27]

In May 1868, through the efforts of Mrs. Eliza Potter, a native of Rhode Island who had moved to Charleston with her businessman husband before the Civil War, the soldiers were reinterred at Beaufort and Florence National Cemeteries or in their home communities. Mrs. Potter, a Unionist, had nursed the soldiers in Hampton Park. Mrs. Potter was buried in a national cemetery in recognition of her efforts on behalf of the Union soldiers and her advocacy for a national system of cemeteries for soldiers.

Chapter 6
AFTER THE WAR

By 1866, the Jockey Club was advertising the Washington Race Course for lease as farmland. On November 23, 1868, a letter to the editor in the local paper mourned the passing of the old racecourse days. The author incorrectly stated that "a gallant Virginian who had fought for liberty and South Carolina with distinguished honor in the Revolutionary War" had given the Jockey Club the land for the racecourse. He noted that the Civil War had taken a heavy toll on the people of Charleston, nearly wiping out even the racers themselves: "[F]or not content with other spoils, the enemy even sought out these…" In addition, the growth of the city itself was inching toward the old racecourse. Therefore, the editorial suggested the land should perhaps be returned to the family of its Virginian donor.[28]

Although the Jockey Club did not accept the invitation to give up the racecourse, the club did explore other options. In December 1848, a group of gentlemen had met to discuss the possibility of holding an agricultural and industrial fair to show off the area's potential and introduce new technology. Their group was known as the South Carolina Institute, and they held their first fair in the fall of 1849 at Military Hall. The group had succeeded enough to construct a notable headquarters on Meeting Street (present-day 141 Meeting Street) by 1853, but the hall and all of its records were destroyed by the Great Fire of 1861. The Civil War added to the woes of the group, and the annual fair was nearly snuffed out.[29]

In February 1870, however, at a meeting at Market Hall, the board of the South Carolina Institute announced that the tradition would be revived with a fair held in November and lasting several days. To hold a fair would require large amounts of land for field tests and buildings, but the South Carolina Jockey Club had agreed to collaborate. The cost of the fair was estimated at $15,000, and the proposal was unanimously endorsed.[30]

Plans were underway right off. By September 1870, buildings were largely in place. The main building, built by G.W. Egan, backed up to Rutledge Avenue and stood nearly in the location of what is today The Citadel softball stadium's third-base bleachers. The building was three hundred feet long by eighty feet wide by forty feet tall with 154 windows, 14 doors and a ten-foot-wide piazza overlooking the racecourse, which would be put in good order for races again.

The interior was one grand room, well ventilated, with windows spaced at four feet. A ladies' parlor was enclosed inside the entrance and another room for meetings on the opposite side. Throughout the main building and around the grounds of the old racecourse, national and state flags were flown, and garlands and displays of greenery and flowers filled the exhibition space. Upon entering the main building, visitors were treated to an open work iron fountain designed and made by famous ironworker Christopher Werner. It rose from a circular basin about ten feet across and shot a spray of water high into the air, where the droplets then helped cool the room.

The South Carolina Institute Fair opened on November 1, 1870, with a hearty endorsement by the *Charleston Daily News*: "Charleston will do her part in the grand work of building up South Carolina, and extends a cordial welcome to all her visitors, whether they come from North or West or South. There is no sectionalism in commerce, and we can promise to all who now pay our city a visit a hearty and generous reception."[31]

Open from nine o'clock to five o'clock each day, the fair was open to all, white and black, with no distinction of race made. At first, the city railway was not expected to be extended from Rutledge Avenue, and there was a fear that that would hurt attendance. That matter was later reversed, and thousands of people bought daily tickets for twenty-five cents. On just one day, more than twelve thousand people streamed to the racecourse to see the spectacle.

Inside the exhibition hall was a dizzying array of sights. There were twenty-four tables on which all manner of goods were displayed, ranging from baking powder and false teeth to agricultural equipment and sewing machines. A steam engine was installed to keep all of the apparatuses spinning.[32] In addition to the practical, visitors enjoyed seeing the merely interesting and beautiful. One organizer arranged to have a fire truck on display, and many Charlestonians contributed artwork. Ex-governor William

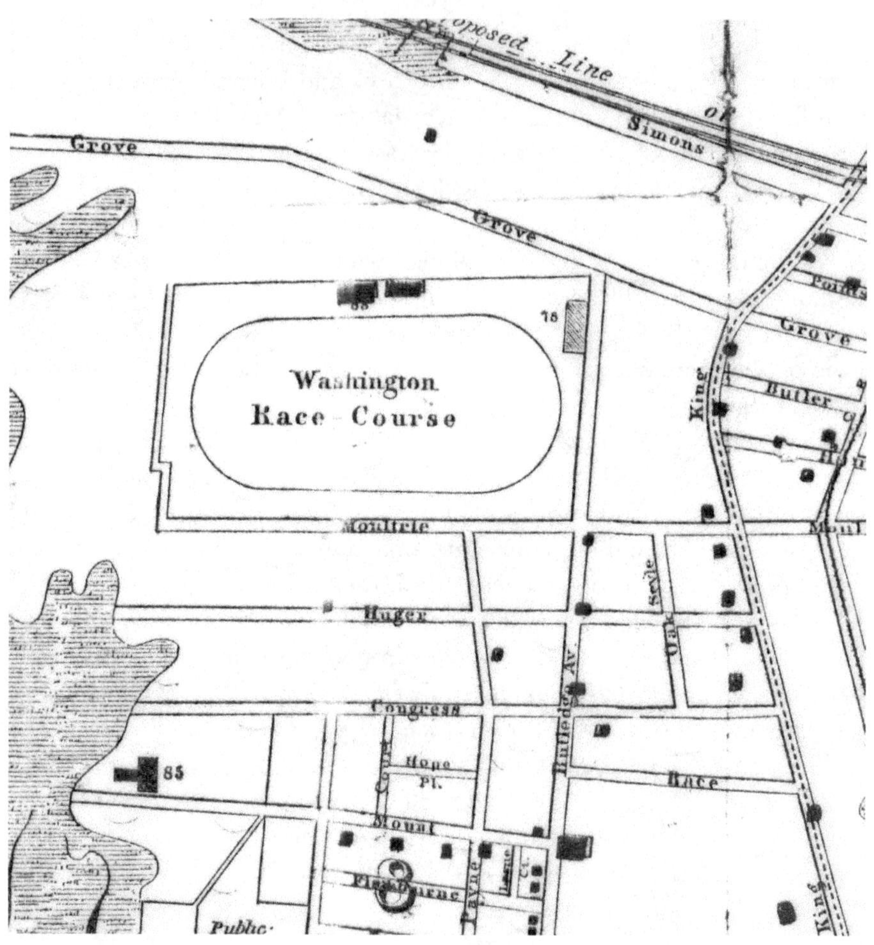

This city map was prepared in 1879 and is the only known image showing the display hall for the South Carolina Institute. According to the map's legend, the structure was used as a public school in that year. *Charleston County Library, South Carolina Room.*

Aiken exhibited some art, including a madonna and child in the style of Raphael and a painting of Romeo and Juliet by Lester Terry from the art gallery at his home, the Aiken-Rhett House at 48 Elizabeth Street.

Two stairways led to the piazza where throngs of people could watch the events playing out on the old Washington Race Course. Many horse races were held, but other events were staged too, including footraces. On one afternoon, a parade of horsemen in armor entered the course carrying banners in the style of a medieval tournament. They held contests, including lancing at rings. J.M. Nelson, competing as the "Knight of Kingstree," won the tournament and, after due pomp, was given the chance to pick the Queen of the Fair.[33]

While the newspapers gushed about the success of the fair, not everything was a hit with the reporters.[34] The *Daily News* reported its disapproval of one ghastly event in which the competitors tried to jerk the head from a live goose:

> *This was a species of sport which we sincerely trust will never again be incorporated in the amusements of the day. It exercised our most sovereign disgust, and was an exhibition of cruelty unfit for the occasion…* [A] *live gander has his feathers stripped off his neck down to his breast, his bare part is then well greased, and, while suspended by the feet from a tree, attempts were made by mounted men to pull the head from the body. Four or five attempts were made in this direction, and after fruitless attempts to take the head off, the poor thing was jerked down, and swung about into the air until it was tortured to death. The man who accomplished the feat should certainly consider it a mean honor.*[35]

The center of the racecourse was used for plowing demonstrations and crop displays. Like a state fair, there were equal parts education and amusement, and music was offered at a bandstand.[36] Alcoholic beverages were not permitted on the grounds, but the old Jockey Club grandstands were retained and operated as a saloon. Between the Jockey Club grandstands and the Exhibition Hall was a carnival atmosphere with hawkers trying to lure people into tents to see sword-swallowers and bearded ladies.[37]

The fair had been so popular during its initial run of November 1 through November 5 that the organizers extended the event, and it concluded on November 8, 1870. A baseball game was played at the end of the day. Only three innings were played because of a late start following other events, but the score was already 27–16 with the Palmettos leading the Schachte team. The fair was regarded as quite a success: "And now the great fair of the South Carolina Institute is over. A brilliant and well-deserved success has crowned the persistent and untiring efforts of the board of directors of the Institute and of those herculean workers, the board of manager of the fair, to whom the well-done of an appreciative community is justly rendered."[38]

With the course back in condition, a last gasping effort to revive horse racing was made, and a few races were held. Still, horse racing never took off again after the Civil War, and the South Carolina Jockey Club limped along. The Jockey Club was very particular about the horses that it would allow to race, and the club also did not permit harness racing. The trade-off of maintaining its strong positions was that the final races were held in February 1882, and the club stopped accepting new members. With time, the membership dwindled, and by the end of the century, there were only twenty-six members. As explained by the president of the club:

> *After a full and fair trial in successive years, it was clearly proved that the spirit of racing in this locality, as it had existed throughout the history and life of the South Carolina Jockey Club down to the beginning of the war between the States, had died out in the land. Patrons of the races, and horse owners and breeders, such as had represented the club from far back in the last century, were few and far between. Attendance of ladies and gentlemen from all parts of the State and from the City of Charleston had almost wholly ceased. Even the patronage of the humble citizens was no longer what it had been, and the old resource of "gate money" had fallen away almost entirely. It was found that the debt of the club was increasing yearly and that we were running races at a loss. The club decided to give up racing.*

There had been some discussion of disbanding and donating the club's assets for about two years. One idea had been to donate the assets to the City of Charleston, but the members worried that their gift would be "lost sight of" in the general budget of the city and would be "the object of game for politicians," who would try to use it for purposes inconsistent with the club's wishes. The president of the club, Major Theodore Barker, came up with the idea of donating the assets to the Charleston Library Society. A special meeting was held on December 29, 1899, and members voted to disband the South Carolina Jockey Club and donate the club's property to the South Carolina Library Society for the creation of an endowment. The resolution summarized the problem the members faced: "[T]he prospects of the amusement of horse racing on a respectable and financially safe footing have proved to be hopeless and the South Carolina Jockey Club finds itself the owner of property which can no longer be utilized for the purpose for which it was formed…"[39]

The cash and investments of the club were valued at about $13,000, but the total value of the gift, including the racecourse and its improvements, was about $100,000.

The gateposts at the entrance to the Washington Race Course were the final remnants of the once-great track. They remained for a few years after the dissolution of the South Carolina Jockey Club. Although horse racing had disappeared from Charleston's popular culture, wealthy industrialists in the North picked up the sport. In the winter, they needed a warmer location than Long Island in which to keep their Thoroughbreds and train them. Some horses were shipped to Oakland or New Orleans, but the best of an owner's horses were kept in the Northeast over winter.

Some horse owners had stabled their Thoroughbreds in Charleston at least for a few years. William Collins Whitney of New York was one of the first to begin the interest in overwintering horses in the South, when he established a home in the Winter Colony in Aiken, South Carolina. In 1902, Whitney instructed his local agents to expand his operations in Aiken so that he could ship his entire stable of horses south for the winter.[40]

That same season, August Belmont, also of New York, wintered his horses in Garnett, South Carolina. Belmont maintained a private, three-quarter-mile track there. Others considered nearby Summerville as a cold weather haven: "[W]hen the snow flies in the East the best of the high class race class horses will be basking in the Southern sunlight."

At the same time that Belmont was stabling his horses in South Carolina, he was planning what would be the largest horse-racing facility in the country in New York. The $5 million track and stables would later bear its builder's name as Belmont Park. Belmont must have visited Charleston and learned of the old gateposts of the old Washington Race Course. The four posts "of prodigious size" were made of brick and weighed about ten tons each.[41] One travel journalist described encountering the posts in 1895: "Just outside the city limits we find a pair of stone posts standing alone in the middle of a cultivated field, indicating where once gathered the wealth and fashion of the country upon the Washington Race Track."[42]

In 1903, the City of Charleston gave the entrance gateposts to Belmont to install at Belmont Park. The posts were lowered in one piece and not disassembled apparently, as a newspaper account tells of one unfortunate worker's having "the life mashed out of him" when a guy wire slipped and the column crushed William Mosimann. Today, the posts are located on an automobile entrance to the Belmont Park clubhouse, where they are not frequently noted by visitors. A plaque, however, does note their historical significance.

The donation of the pillars was not warmly endorsed by Charleston. A few days after the newspaper first broke the news that the park commissioners had given the pillars away, another article reported the differences between the culture of Charleston's old racing community and the sordid, gambling culture of northern racetracks. Following the report, a "letter to the editor"

Long after the last races at the Washington Race Course, the gateposts of the entrance remained until they were shipped to Belmont Park in New York. In the 1910s, new posts, inspired by these originals, were built to mark the entrance to the new neighborhood going in just south of the park, Hampton Park Terrace. (George Marshall Allan, "Charleston: A Typical City of the South," *Magazine of Travel*, January 1895.)

A plaque was added to one of the historic posts from the Washington Race Course when they were reinstalled at the entrance to Belmont Park in New York in 1903. *The New York Racing Association, Inc.*

was printed signed with the name "McChesney," a nom de plume for an anonymous columnist of the paper. Assuming that the tone was meant as utterly sarcastic, his opinion was bitter. After questioning what possible practical use the gates could serve, the author closed with this:

> *It seems to me that we have relics to burn. It has been said that we have too much history and too many landmarks. We should be glad that Mr. Belmont has accepted the brick pillars and we might give away the old City Wall, the old Postoffice* [sic], *the Powder Magazine and a score of other relics that hamper our progress. Let us "cut out" this ancient business and send our relics to the block. As a sporting man I am truly glad the old gates will go to Belmont Park. Send those other moth-eaten objects with it and let us go after business.*[43]

The next day, the Charleston newspaper ran three letters to the editors that took the park commission to task for giving away Charleston's "birthright" without even having the excuse of filling the municipal coffers. The pillars were described as "valued souvenirs of past peculiarities of a peculiar people" and "relics of a glorious past." One letter, signed by "Some Colonial Dames," asked, "Would it not have been better to scatter the bricks of the old gate posts, rather than have them erected elsewhere as monuments to the stupidity which will be ascribed, not to the park commissioners, but to the entire community?"[44]

While Charlestonians were unhappy, the matter was finally resolved at a city council meeting on April 28, 1903. Councilman Samuel Lapham, the head of the park commission, explained that Belmont had sought the gates, which were in poor repair, and had promised to place them in a prominent spot with appropriate plaques marking their significance. The park commissioners had accepted the offer, thinking it was appropriate for the old pillars. A different account had appeared in the *New York Times*, which reported that Belmont had offered to buy the pillars but that the "city was not willing to place a money valuation on the property, and it was presented to Belmont with the compliments of the city."[45] Regardless, Councilman Frost noted that the park commissioners had not had the authority to dispose of the posts. Councilman Lapham proposed approving the gift after the fact, and all but one councilman voted in favor of it. So ended the long history of the Washington Race Course.

Chapter 7

THE SOUTH CAROLINA INTERSTATE AND WEST INDIAN EXPOSITION

The idea of a major trade exposition to promote Charleston was first floated by Colonel John H. Averill during a meeting meant to organize Charleston's Fall Festival. The annual fall event typically involved parades and perhaps a traveling show or circus. A block of Calhoun Street or another street in the commercial district would be closed for a few days, and stores had sales. But at a meeting on October 2, 1899, Colonel Averill took the floor and suggested rethinking the Fall Festival and expanding it into a first-rate trade exposition of national scope. The newspaper captured his remarks:

> *Why not change the Fall Festival to an Exposition of the resources and industry of South Carolina. Abandon the Festival this year, and open the twentieth century, one year from now, with an Exposition that will reflect credit on our city and all its people. It can be done: you have undertaken and carried through more difficult tasks. I consider one of the grandest opportunities ever offered is yours. There is no agency so effective in bringing about good and great results as a creditable Exposition. The resources and possibilities of our State are large. The products of our waters, fields and forests will make no inconsiderable display, and our industries are rapidly bringing the State into greater and greater importance with those who have capital to invest, and who are especially concerned in the development of industrial enterprises. I believe that the people of the whole State would cheerfully co-operate with us in making such an Exposition a success.*[46]

The *Charleston News & Courier* heartily endorsed the idea, and its editorial page called for work to begin immediately on an exposition to occur at the new Thompson Auditorium at present-day Cannon Park: "There will be a great deal of work to be done, and there is no better time to begin it than the present." Whether the newspaper was reporting popular support for the movement or causing it is hard to say, but popular support swelled quickly. The Young Men's Business League took up the idea during a meeting at the Charleston Hotel, and a special committee was appointed to investigate the matter. A week later, the committee reported back favorably on the possibility, and $1,500 was raised to begin the groundwork. The statehouse passed a resolution supporting the idea in January 1900. The City of Charleston followed suit, and Mayor J. Adger Smyth endorsed the plans on March 29, 1900. Already by that time, the organizers had raised $40,000. A corporation was created to pursue the matter, including leading businessmen and politicians as its incorporators, and Captain F.W. Wagener was chosen as the company's chairman.

Outside Charleston, sentiment was more cautious. As one Vermont monthly said, "The audacity of this little town in sandwiching in an exposition between the great fairs of Buffalo and St. Louis is truly great."[47] Nevertheless, by May 4, 1900, the total backing for the idea amounted to $116,415. A delegation was dispatched to New York to subscribe railroads and succeeded wildly, with the South Atlantic Line and the Plant System Railways contributing a total of $40,000. The Clyde Steamship Line contributed $2,500. By June, the company had already subscribed shares worth $178,790 at that point, and most were bought by people of moderate means.[48]

Work progressed quickly, and by late summer, the board of directors of the new South Carolina, Interstate and West Indian Exposition Co. had already begun construction plans. At a special meeting held on August 4, 1900, the board of directors selected Bradford Lee Gilbert of New York as the architect for the exposition. Gilbert graduated from Yale in 1875 before joining a firm in New York City. While in New York, his work focused on large, commercial and institutional buildings, especially train depots, including the Mexican National Railway terminals in Mexico City and the Illinois Central depot. He had also designed some of the buildings at the Chicago World's Fair and had served as the chief architect of the 1895 Atlanta Exposition. Not just an architect, he was also something of an engineer who had gained prominence for developing the "skeleton framing" method, which greatly increased floor space inside skyscrapers. His technique would be put to use in designing the massive, but largely hollow, display halls at the Charleston Exposition.[49]

Gilbert's choice of style bore absolutely no relation to Charleston's architectural history, but the theme was liked: "In working out his conception, the Architect gave primary importance and emphasis throughout to what he described in professional language as 'a typical Southern character and motif,' and it was because of the fidelity with which he held to his original and single idea, that the Colonial South and Ancient Spain blended in building, and landscape, and vista in a way that was fascinating beyond description."

Samuel H. Wilson was in charge of the committee reviewing sites and decided the best location would be the old Washington Race Course grounds and the adjacent Rhett Farm between the track and the Ashley River. The Rhett Farm, however, had tenant farmers on it who would not agree to leave, so instead the grounds reached northward and took advantage of Captain Wagener's own land. With a few additions around the edges, the final grounds included about 250 acres. Gilbert divided the lands into two sections: The Washington Race Course would follow a highly structured, formal layout, and Wagener's northern lands would use a natural layout. As Hemphill later wrote, "[W]hile the birds bands were playing in the grand Court of Palaces, the birds were singing in the trees of the Farm."[50]

Ground was broken on December 11, 1900, at a huge public gathering at which the governor and mayor both spoke. The crowds began arriving four hours before the opening ceremonies were set to begin and began making themselves comfortable for the wait, enjoying glorious, cool, sunny weather.[51] Throngs of people walked from Marion Square behind a parade of Citadel cadets, students from the Porter Military Academy and other civilian military groups. Leading the way was South Carolina governor M.B. McSweeney. Five hundred took part and marched to the truck fields near Grove Street, where the exposition's buildings would soon go up. Carriages and bicycles brought more people, and the trolley system had special rides scheduled during the afternoon, which were packed. By the time the ceremonies started, there were approximately seven to eight thousand people in attendance.

The main platform, decked out in red, white and blue, contained seating for the exposition's officers and directors, more than one hundred distinguished guests and a chorus. It was decorated with palmetto fronds and flags hung from an arch over the platform. The dignitaries all took their positions as artillery booms announced the arrival of the governor. At last, the rector of St. Michael's Episcopal offered a prayer, and the event was underway.

Captain Wagener took the stage in his full German Artillery uniform and greeted the crowd with a smile that "seemed to broaden out into a personal greeting to every man, woman and child within the gates of the grounds."

New York architect Bradford Gilbert's use of blended Spanish Colonial and Renaissance Revival styles for the exposition's main buildings was inexplicably described as typically southern. Individual states hired their own architects to design their buildings, resulting in even more dissimilar (but interesting) designs. *Drawing by Bradford Gilbert.*

Mayor Smyth was recognized and reminded the crowd of the purpose of the venture: "It is to place before the world, not only the products of our soil and our manufacturers, but also to demonstrate what wonderful unoccupied fields are here ready for the remunerative employment of the abundant capital which all over our land is seeking investment."

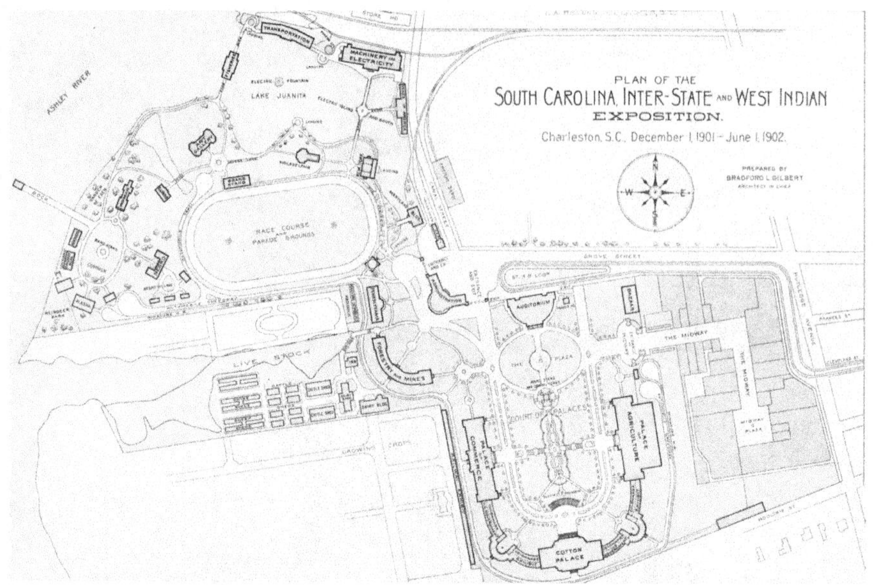

A naturalistic portion of the exposition grounds was built on Captain Wagener's own property, Lowndes Grove Plantation. The more formal portion to the south and the adjacent midway attractions became Hampton Park after the exposition closed in 1902. *Drawing by Bradford Gilbert.*

Following the speeches, the local Freemasons performed a ceremony before the setting of the cornerstone of the first building, the Administration Building. A copper box was placed in the cornerstone that contained the following: copies of the local newspapers; a list of the exposition's officers; specimens of Georgia pine, marble and granite; a copy of the *Atlanta Constitution*; and a document from the Freemasons. The Administration Building would be the first building completed in September 1901.

After laying the cornerstone of the Administration Building, work started on other aspects of the project. The excavation of the Lake and Sunken Gardens started in February 1901, and by May 1, 1901, new lines of the Consolidated Railroad were in place. The three main buildings around the Sunken Gardens included the central Cotton Palace (built by the City of Charleston), the Palace of Agriculture (built by the State of South Carolina) and the Palace of Commerce (built by the exposition company itself). The three buildings totaled 100,000 square feet of space more than had been at the Pan-American Exposition. They required 2.5 million feet of lumber and 60 tons of nails. The entire collection of buildings was painted an off-white using automatic painting machines to cover the twenty acres of surface. While the majority of the surface might have been ivory, the buildings were not just giant, white-washed structures. Instead, the buildings had delicate, colored metalwork and richly painted panels, cornices and columns using reds, browns and yellows.[52] The result was popularly known as the "Ivory City."

The Cotton Palace was the central building of the exposition, and it was immense. Inside were displays of King Cotton in all of its many forms and the machinery that was used to make fabrics. Cotton-seed oil, cooking compounds and soap were all on display.

In the natural portion of the grounds on Captain Wagener's land, the buildings were much more unique. Buildings were dedicated to topics and to specific demonstrators. There was a Maryland Building, a New York Building, a Philadelphia Building, a Fine Arts Building, an Alaska Building, a Cincinnati Building, a Woman's Building (the old Lowndes Grove plantation house) and a Louisiana Purchase Building. The buildings displayed Colonial, Mission and other styles. The buildings were, for the most part, not display galleries but were instead designed to house offices of the various state and city delegations.

Other buildings displayed materials on a particular theme unconnected to a special location. A fisheries exhibit displayed aquaculture information, for instance. In the Negro Building, a display was set out that would demonstrate the advances of African Americans. The display had been overseen by Booker T. Washington, who had visited Charleston in September to make final arrangements.[53] In a sad and ironic turn of events, one of the sculptors for the exposition had used Washington as the basis for one of the figures in a large statue to be placed in front of the Negro Building.[54] The statue, however artistic, played to the worst stereotypes of the day; the figures showed, among others, a young man sitting on a bale of cotton, playing a banjo and singing while another carried a basket of cotton on her head. Objections from the Negro Department led to its removal to another spot on the fairgrounds.

Covering many of the buildings were pieces of highly decorative (but fleeting) staff, a plaster-like material. The staff work was done on the fairgrounds and overseen by John Fredericks and Paul Grandmougin, expert modelers, and performed by locals. The staff work was not limited to the architectural, though. Spread around the grounds were artistic works, both original and reproductions, that were executed in the same staff. Some works were brought in, including the sculptural groups from the Dewey Triumphal Arch in New York, which the City Council of New York had given to the exposition for display on the Fine Arts Building.

The grounds of the exposition were full of staff statuary. A workshop was set up with the latest replication machinery, which allowed small models to

The Cotton Palace was the central display building at the exposition. Alone, it required 600,000 feet of lumber. It was 320 feet long and 185 feet high. *College of Charleston.*

The main display buildings surrounded an area known as the Court of Palaces. In the center, the land was excavated for a lagoon with an island full of flowers and shrubs connected to the mainland by four ornate bridges. Although the buildings are gone, the Sunken Gardens remain (albeit in highly modified form) as the focal point of Hampton Park today. *College of Charleston.*

The Liberty Bell was shipped to Charleston for display in the Philadelphia exhibit, a 120- by 80-foot structure, and celebrated on January 9, 1902, with Liberty Bell Day at the exposition. *College of Charleston.*

One of the more fanciful buildings at the exposition was Pennsylvania's. Designed by Phil H. Johnson, the Spanish Renaissance building was 150 feet long and 80 feet wide with a 12-foot piazza surrounding it and a semicircular court. *College of Charleston.*

State and city buildings, unlike the exposition's main galleries, were as varied as the places they represented. The Louisiana Purchase Building was a Dutch Colonial, the Cincinnati Building was a Spanish Colonial and Alaska was represented by a log cabin and tower. *From promotional materials for the South Carolina Interstate and West Indian Exposition.*

Booker T. Washington helped develop a display meant to show the progress of blacks in the South. *University of South Carolina, Caroliniana Library.*

be enlarged quite easily. Directing the device toward a small version of the work would then cause another part of the machine to point to the same point on a larger scale—much like a signing machine. The cost of large-scale works was reduced to a mere 20 percent of what it might have cost without the equipment. In addition to the main groups, the shop produced a stag to be placed at Lake Juanita, cupids for the Lovers' Lane portion of the grounds and birds and alligators to fill in.[55]

The staff work at the exposition was so plentiful that there were three buildings on-site dedicated to its production during the summer of 1901. The chief architect's offices prepared exacting drawings of all of the work and submitted them to the workshops. There, workmen created clay models of each piece and allowed them to harden under a coating of varnish. Gelatin molds were then produced and used to replicate hundreds of pieces each. Larger details would include a wooden center or some reinforcing material, such as bagging remnants and hemp. The final pieces were then all painted by a machine instead of by hand.[56]

No less impressive were the grounds themselves. The garden design was created by Anton Fiehe. Lake Juanita, the central feature of the natural grounds, was formed by damming a tidal creek, and industrial buildings were built around it. Decorative bridges spanned the lake, and a pavilion known as the Electrical Booth, built on a man-made island in the center, was illuminated with electric lights.[57] An electric fountain in Lake Juanita threw water in several jets to a point atop the Electrical Booth. The water then cascaded down the stained-glass walls of the building before being drawn back into a fountain inside the structure.

Visitors could enjoy the grounds both day and night because of the extensive electrical lighting plans. Samuel Lapham, a member of city council and a board member, was placed in charge of plans. He used a combination of arc lights and incandescent lights to illuminate both the interiors of buildings and their exteriors. The undertaking was large enough that the Charleston Consolidated Railway, Gas and Electric Co. built a plant on the grounds. The powerhouse contained thirteen enormous General Electric generators, which fed power to a control station located at the top of the auditorium. From there, a concert of lighting played out each night as lights were slowly turned on around the Sunken Gardens in a display unlike any that had ever been seen in Charleston before.[58]

Around the northeastern portion of the current Hampton Park was a midway, which provided relief from the educational components of the exposition with a variety of amusing rides and displays.[59] The midway was not unique to the Charleston Exposition; like a modern carnival, the concessionaires completed their run at the Buffalo Pan-American Exposition in early November 1901, packed up their outfits, shipped everything to Charleston and rebuilt the same exhibits.[60] Although the midway took up about thirty acres, work was barely started until less than one month before the opening day.

Another feature of the exposition meant for entertainment and not education was a racecourse. When the Washington Race Course closed, a smaller, private track was developed on the land of exposition chairman Captain Wagener. The track was a half-mile course. The exposition organizers sold the racing rights for $37,500, and a syndicate then organized a series of daily races at the track. New grandstands were built, the existing track was improved and stables for five hundred horses were added nearby.[61] The first races were held on December 16, 1901, and then daily (except Sunday) with five purses totaling $1,000. A small admission was charged for entry to the grandstands so "undesirable characters may be discouraged from entering."[62] The "undesirables" perhaps attended the races in any event, and at least one "blind tiger" was suspected of operating in a restaurant near the course.[63] The racecourse ultimately did not succeed. The Eastern Jockey Club voted to expel members who took part in the Charleston races, and the field of horses dwindled to the point that full races could not be scheduled.[64]

The big day finally arrived on December 2, 1901, and the gates were thrown open for regular business. A parade one mile long led from Marion Square to the exposition grounds. At 1:20 p.m., the Huguenot Church's pastor delivered an invocation to start the ceremonies in the auditorium. A special wire had been set up so that the local dignitaries could telegraph their greetings to President Roosevelt in Washington. The president responded a few moments later, "America" was performed, a forty-six-gun salute was fired and the exposition was officially open. On the opening day of the exposition in December 1901, twenty-two thousand people went through the turnstiles to enjoy sights and sounds like they had never seen or heard.

Throughout the exposition, there were special days marked on the calendar. The list of common denominators that merited a special day was long enough that almost every day seems to have been used to honor some group or another. One, however, made a greater splash than all the others. April 9, 1902, was designated as "President's Day" at the exposition to celebrate the visit of President Theodore Roosevelt. The official delegation had arrived outside the city by train from Washington, D.C., and then took a ship to Charleston. It was heralded as the "greatest day in half a century of Charleston's history."

A parade of three thousand representatives of all branches of the state and federal military marched to the exposition while thousands of people

Part carnival, part exotic display, the midway included Eskimos from Greenland, dancers from the West Indies and many exotic displays from all points in between. Visitors could see Bostock's Animal Show, the "Streets of Cairo," a cyclorama of the Battle of Bull Run, an "upside down" house, a temple of palmistry and other exotic and amusing diversions. *From promotional materials for the South Carolina Interstate and West Indian Exposition.*

A new racecourse was constructed on the grounds of Captain F.W. Wagener's home, Lowndes Grove, for the exposition, which continued the tradition of horse races on the upper peninsula. *University of South Carolina, Caroliniana Library.*

crowded the sidewalks and streets all along the route. When the throngs reached the grounds, President Roosevelt went to the auditorium where the troops then gathered for a military review that lasted about thirty minutes. The president then took to the stage in the auditorium and began an address that combined praise for Charleston, support for American foreign policy and a strong theme of North-South reconciliation.[65] Following his speech and a brisk walk through some of the exhibition halls, the presidential party was taken to the Women's Department at Lowndes Grove Plantation, where a fine luncheon was served. From lunch, the president was taken to the Fine Arts Building, where he spent some time taking in the city hall collection. The presidential party was then escorted to the train depot at the edge of the exposition, where a train was waiting to take the party to Summerville, where Captain Wagener entertained them at his Pine Forest Inn.

Individuals could attend the exposition for a day, of course, but the exposition also offered unlimited passes, which permitted holders to come to the grounds every day. At first, the unlimited passes cost $10.00, but as the exposition wore on, the rate was cut in half in hopes of boosting attendance. Between December 1, 1901, and May 31, 1902, there were a total of 674,086 guests. Of those, just over half were multiday passes, while about 321,000 were regular admissions at the various gates and at various rates. The total income from tickets was $148,062.90.

For more than a year, organizers had been promoting the exposition to anyone who would listen. The newspaper (with its close ties to the board of directors of the exposition) temporarily suspended journalistic principles and became a glorified commercial for the exposition. Every day, articles raved about exciting news from the fairgrounds and kept the matter in everyone's consciousness. And there is at least some reason to think that the unrelenting boosterism worked at first. Captain Peter Toglio, a retired mariner, for example, took up the challenge to prepare more housing for the waves of tourists who were expected with what must be one of the most unusual buildings ever built in Charleston: At his home at the corner of Rutledge Avenue and Cannon Street, Captain Toglio built a hotel in the form of a steamship. The building, with housing for about fifty, would be 125 feet long and 25 feet wide with a gracefully curved bow, a smokestack and even a "ragman," a sort of scarecrow, placed at the helm. The entire structure was surrounded with an excavated pond six inches deep to give the appearance of a Dutch galleon at port. Sadly, although a newspaper column described the building in progress, there are no known photographs showing the resulting hotel, christened "The Exposition."

Captain Toglio's imaginative efforts to capitalize on the great fair might have been scuttled when turnout was lower than anticipated. In the end, attendance for the exposition was described as "pitifully small."[66] One visitor wrote, "It is amusing to see the tradesmen and shouters of the Midway pounce upon the few straggling visitors to sell them their oriental wares or inveigle them into their show-tents covered with flaming signs." The possible causes of the low attendance were many: the exposition was not well advertised, Charleston was just too far off the beaten path and people were just tired of too many expositions. Organizers of the exposition groused that the lack of federal support was to blame; not only did Congress refuse to contribute money, but also the lack of federal support (especially after its enthusiastic support for the Buffalo Exposition) gave the impression that the Charleston exposition was second-rate by comparison.

The organizers of the exposition never wavered in their enthusiasm for the fair, even after it had ended in failure. Rather than blaming their own planning miscues, the cause of the low ticket sales, in their estimation, was something beyond their control: the weather. As Hemphill remembered it later, "So long a period of continuous cold, extending as it did, over a period of more than three months, was one of the distresses against which the Exposition authorities could not provide. Weeks, that were so cold that the Esquimaux themselves found the conditions most uncomfortable, passed, and naturally during all this time the attendance was not such as the excellence of the attractions warranted."[67]

The final day of the exposition was May 31, 1902, celebrated as "Charleston Day," with speeches galore and pomp and circumstance everywhere. Mock battles were fought, dances were held and music filled the air. Throngs of attendees filled the Sunken Gardens with picnics in the afternoon to hear the last band performance before dispersing to take in the final shows. At the stroke of midnight, a shot was fired, "Taps" was played and the exposition drew to a close.[68]

Over the next several months, creditors of the exposition made applications through the court for funds owed. On July 2, 1902, after diligent lobbying, Congress eventually authorized a federal bailout of $160,000 to help resolve the outstanding claims against the exposition. If the money was inadequate, it was suggested that the receivers would sort through the claims and prorate the federal funds.[69] When the exposition was first planned, it was expected that the United States would contribute $250,000 to the venture; it did not, but the organizers had already planned on a scope based on this assumption. By the end of the lawsuits, creditors received about 65 percent of their money back on the failed venture.[70]

One of the only physical assets of the exposition was the collection of buildings and the physical materials on the exposition grounds. On July 31, 1902, a public auction was held for almost all of the exposition property.[71] Eighty-nine potential bidders (including "three small boys and one decrepit old negro") showed up for the auction. Entire buildings were sold off for $115; some were sold for as little as $7. Even showcase buildings like the Palace of Commerce brought just $105. Fences, ticket booths, stables, grandstands and even underground pipes were all sold to the highest bidder. Most of the buyers were contractors or businesses, and they purchased on the condition that the property be removed promptly. Even the newspaper struck a sentimental note about the sale: "So the work of demolition will be prosecuted now with all possible speed. In a few days the beautiful Ivory City will be a heap of lumber and debris and every vestige of its splendor will be blotted from the things that be."

In just over two hours, almost the entire exposition had gone under the hammer. The State Building was exempt because it belonged to the state, and the Cotton Palace was exempt because it belonged to the City of Charleston. The sale generated $10,105.50. A few days later, the personal property—buckets, towels, chairs, tables and other miscellaneous items—was sold in a second auction totaling $2,000.00.[72]

The demolition of the exposition started immediately. In less than a week after the sale, many of the buildings had been torn down and teamsters were busy carting away the lumber and debris. The purchaser of the underground pipes had already dug up some of his property and left the grounds scarred with crisscrossing trenches. "The hand of the destroyer [was] apparent everywhere."[73]

The demolition process lasted several months. The last of the buildings that had been sold off for demolition did not come down until the spring of 1903. A Philadelphia contractor had been given the contracts for the large-scale demolition and salvage of the Cotton Palace and Administration Building, and he used a chain gang to perform some of the work. Most of the good-quality materials were loaded onto trains and shipped to Philadelphia for use in other buildings, but some were sold locally.[74]

The buildings on the exposition grounds had been extraordinary—or at least extraordinary looking. Despite their monumental size and elaborate decoration, they were never meant to be permanent. One exception was the Palace of the Arts. The classically styled building was built of solid brick to provide a fireproof showplace for paintings and statutory imported from far and near. The building exhibited statuary of some historical note: Four large

Charleston's city council offered part of its own art collection from city hall, including its famous portrait of George Washington. *From promotional materials for the South Carolina Interstate and West Indian Exposition.*

groups of statues were saved from Dewey's Arch in New York, a monument meant to honor Admiral George Dewey, which had been destroyed on November 26, 1900. Notable artists whose works were on display included John Audubon, Rembrandt Peale, Gilbert Stuart, Thomas Sully, Mary Cassatt, William Merritt Chase, Childe Hassam, Winslow Homer, John Singer Sargent and Frederic Remington. Even after the exposition, the building sat in the middle of pastures as the surrounding acreage returned to agricultural use. It was finally torn down in 1929 for its bricks.

Was the exposition a success? Certainly not financially for the organizers. Captain Wagener himself lost thousands of dollars as a major shareholder, and many creditors never recovered the full amount of their debts. On the other hand, there were some economic benefits for Charleston that should not be written off too quickly. The exposition brought new visitors to Charleston before it was a tourist destination. Housing filled to capacity in downtown as out-of-towners came for the experience. The organizers estimated that $3 million to $5 million was brought into the city by the exposition. Hundreds of jobs were created by the construction and operation of the exposition, and many dignitaries from other states and foreign countries visited along with capitalists looking for expansion opportunities. As it was summed up in a report for Mayor Smyth: "It opened the 'door of opportunity' to our own people, and to those who would come inside this land of promise."

By 1934, the basic layout of Hampton Park was already in place. The Citadel's Parade Grounds are visible near the top of the photograph, the clearing in Hampton Park are the Sunken Gardens, and Mary Murray Boulevard (added in 1924) encircles the park. The remnants of a minor-league baseball field can be picked out at the bottom left corner (McMahon Field today), and the baseball field at the bottom right is College Park today. To the north of Hampton Park (along the right edge), the Wagener Terrace neighborhood was just starting to see construction of its first houses along Grove Street on the former grounds of Lowndes Grove Plantation (barely visible in the extreme, upper-right corner). *The Citadel, the Military College of South Carolina archives.*

Chapter 8

BIRTH OF A PARK

For a city that today takes such great pride in its public spaces, it is hard to believe that little more than a century ago, Charleston had hardly any public parks at all. In fact, after the city created its Board of Park Commissioners in April 1895, the original commissioners noted in their first annual report to Mayor Ficken that there were actually *no parks* under their control. The only traditional public parks—White Point Garden and Colonial Lake—totaled sixteen acres between them, but their operations were entrusted to special boards. Six-acre Marion Square was—and still is—privately owned by the Washington Light Infantry. The total green space open to the public in Charleston, including tiny patches like Wragg Square and Hampstead Mall, amounted to a mere thirty-two acres. But that was soon to change.

The first order of business for the new parks commission was to move forward with a plan for what would have been one of the largest-scaled public parks in South Carolina. In his annual report in March 1896, Mayor Ficken captured this vision for the yet unnamed park: "The tendency in this country is to establish parks outside of the large cities at distances of from five to ten miles, and to connect them with the densely settled portions of the city by broad driveways." That model of parks was fully reflected in the plans developed by the parks commissioners.

The board selected a large parcel along the western bank of the Cooper River about seven miles from city hall. The land had been bought from William Chisolm in February 1895 and had been known as the Retreat

Plantation, later the Turnbull Mansion. The Turnbull House remained, and nearby Marshlands Plantation was also on the site. The property totaled 575 acres, more than two-thirds the size of Central Park in New York City and more than twenty times the size of all other city-owned park space combined.

When Mayor Ficken was replaced by Mayor Adger Smyth, the new administration shared his zeal for the project. In his first annual report in 1896, Mayor Smyth wrote: "No disbursement of public money can give better returns to the entire community than to make attractive, available and enjoyable this beautiful spot, crowned as it is with so many natural advantages and surroundings. It was a wise forethought of the previous administration that secured this ancient and charming family seat for a Charleston park."

The name Chicora Park was adopted at a meeting on December 3, 1895, and work began apace.[75] At one of the very first meetings of the new Board of Park Commissioners, the group decided to hire a "first-class park architect to prepare plans for a park system" and opted for Olmsted, Olmsted & Elliot of Brookline, Massachusetts.

Those Charlestonians who have been aware of the Olmsted connection to Charleston's parks take great pride in the vision for hiring such a notable firm—perhaps too much pride. The Olmsted brothers' landscaping firm was certainly well known by the late nineteenth century, but the people of Charleston can thank Boston's vision, not Charleston's, for making the connection that would, over a forty-year relationship, produce plans for Chicora Park, Hampton Park, Cannon Park and the Ashley riverfront.

On August 16, 1893, the first chairman of the park commission, R.S. Cathcart, wrote a letter to the mayor of Boston asking for help finding a landscape architecture firm to design a park in Charleston. Cathcart included with his correspondence to the mayor a generic letter that explained that Charleston had just purchased "a piece of ground…which we wish laid out for a Park" and wanted to know the price for a set of plans. He asked, with no further information provided, that his enclosed, generic letter requesting those services be passed on by the mayor to "some first class Landscape Architect."

Cathcart did not even know the mayor of Boston. Instead, his letter explained that he had been told by a member of city council of the kindness the mayor had shown to the alderman while on a trip to Boston. He explained that the mayor's kindness "makes me full justified in thinking you would do me this small favor." Cathcart's method of selecting a landscape architect by writing directly and unannounced to the mayor of a major city and asking him to pick a firm for Charleston to use might seem a bit naïve. But it worked. The mayor apparently forwarded both Cathcart's letter and

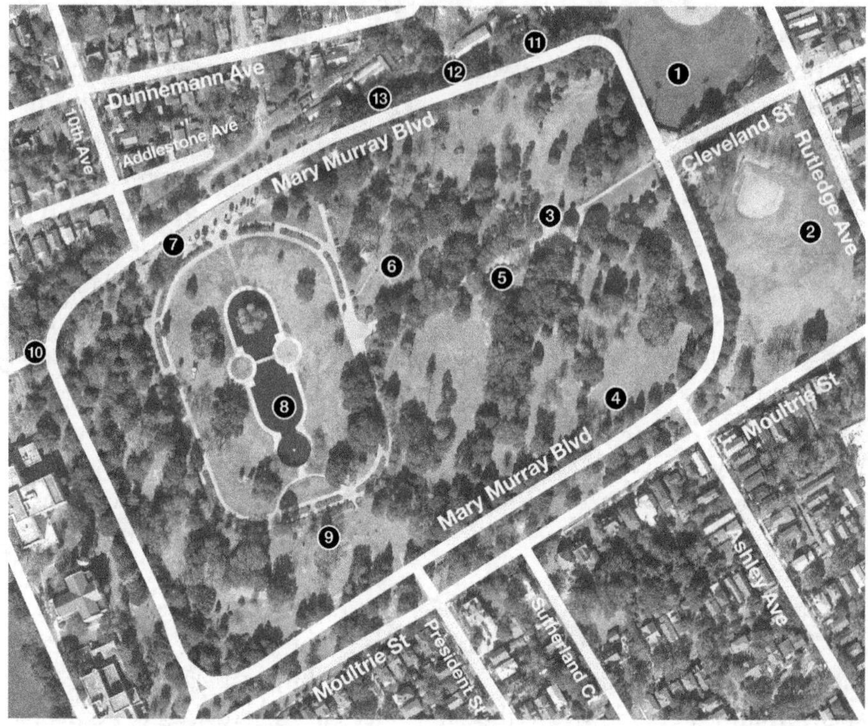

1. College Park (The Citadel softball field)
2. McMahan Playground/Site of Charleston Seagulls minor-league stadium
3. Bandstand/Site of trolley depot
4. Site of Clemson Agricultural Experiment Station (1903–07)
5. Future site of Denmark Vesey statue
6. Pavilion and picnic area
7. Site of Washington Race Course stands and Union burial grounds (approx.)
8. Sunken Gardens
9. Mayor Joseph Riley Jr. monument/Site of Cotton Palace
10. Summerall Gates
11. Colonial Farm House (30 Mary Murray Boulevard)
12. City stables
13. Greenhouses

the generic letter to the Olmsted brothers. Those two letters are the first entries in the Olmsted brothers' file on the Charleston project.

On December 15, 1895, the board agreed to pay the firm fifty dollars and expenses to make the trip to Charleston to view the site. John Olmsted arrived in early 1896 and was taken by the city. When he wrote back to recap his initial thoughts on April 30, 1896, Olmsted's affection for the established, local form was evident:

> *Charleston strikes the visitor from the north as having strongly marked and distinguishing characteristics. Many of these are advisable and would be wise for its citizens to make the most of them. We need only mention in passing the typical residences with 2 or 3 storied side galleries and with fenced yards…filled with southern trees and bushes. It would be a calamity if the citizens do not generally continue this simple and sensible style of house.*

He was especially opposed to eschewing the vernacular style in favor of the "fussy, garish and ephemeral cottage style of our northern cities."

Olmsted was taken by the natural advantages of the location chosen for Chicora Park. He described it as an "admirable piece of ground for a large park" with "beautiful views over the Cooper River" with meadows and a good number of fine trees. "[W]e may say as landscape architects that the city is really fortunate in being surrounded on three sides by salt water with beautiful country beyond it. This being the distinct landscape characteristics of the city it follows that it is the duty of your Board to recognize it to take every possible advantage of it."

Having reviewed his plans, Olmsted responded to the original request for a price for these services: "Our usual charge for park designs varies from $10 per acre for large simple parks, to $20 per acre or more for smaller and more complex parks." He proposed $3,000 plus expenses to design Chicora Park. On June 11, 1896, the parks commission met and agreed to accept the terms, and a contract was completed for services to begin on July 1, 1896. Over the next few years, Chicora Park developed slowly. Plans were made for the restoration of the old plantation house and gardens, a pier was planned for boaters and pleasure drives were laid out.

Unfortunately for Chicora Park, at about the same time, the United States government was considering its options for a new naval facility. After reviewing the merits of Beaufort, South Carolina and Charleston, the government decided that Charleston was the better location. On August

14, 1901, Charleston sold the central part of its riverside parkland to the United States for $200 per acre, a total of more than $34,000.[76] In a separate transaction recorded the same day, the city also sold 760 acres of nearby marshland just south of Chicora Park.[77] The sale of the land indisputably made the most sense for the long-term economic development of the city of Charleston, but Charleston was left without a park.

If the existence of Hampton Park should be credited to any one person, that individual should surely be Samuel Lapham, new chairman of the park commission, who advocated tirelessly for Hampton Park during the next two decades of his public service. When it was clear that Chicora Park was going to be lost, Lapham was already planning on a substitute park that would, in the end, be less ambitious only by comparison to the grand plans for Chicora Park. In his end-of-the-year report for 1901, Lapham wrote the following:

> *The sale to the United States of the entire water front of this park and the tract conveyed extending back 2000 feet from the shores of the Cooper River, as a site for a Naval Station, has taken from this park that part on which all of the improvements had been made under the plans of the Messrs. Olmsted Bros., and the area that possessed most of the great natural beauties which rendered Chicora Park so attractive; and which under the plans for the laying out of this park would have made Chicora Park one of the finest public parks in the United States…*
>
> *Under the circumstances your committee deem it best for the interests of the city and its citizens that a new park site be secured nearer to the city, although it will be impossible to secure a site for a public park in any location adjacent to the city that will have the natural advantages which were possessed by Chicora Park.*[78]

The land that Lapham already envisioned as the replacement for Chicora Park was certainly more convenient, being located at the northern edge of the developed city instead of several miles removed. And the site was similar to Chicora Park in many ways; it enjoyed a fine riverfront location on a bluff overlooking one of Charleston's two rivers and was already served by trolley lines. The only problem was that the land was already being used for a special purpose; the 1901–02 South Carolina Interstate and West Indian Exposition was still in full swing on the land:

> *The nearest site which has a few of the natural beauties of which Chicora Park possessed many, is the Wagener Farm, now occupied by the South*

> *Carolina Inter State and West Indian Exposition Company, and on which the city holds an option, which it would be well to close, and some arrangement be made to secure a few of the buildings thereon owned by the said exposition Company which might be utilized to some advantage in the laying out of the farm as a public park.*[79]

When the exposition closed, the city accepted Chairman Lapham's forward-thinking advice and purchased the land for $32,500 on July 25, 1902.[80]

Early on, Lapham sought to increase the size of the park to take in the waterfront. In his 1903 annual report, he wrote, "It is the purpose of the Board of Park Commission to make this new Park as attractive as possible, considering it is not situated on the Ashley River, but would recommend to City Council that if the same can be secured at a reasonable price, that the intervening tract of land between the present Park and the Ashley River be purchased and made a part of this Park, and thus a water view, so much to be desired, secured." The city agreed on that point and soon started trying to buy the adjacent farmland known as the Rhett Farm, which is today the campus of The Citadel.

Within a short time, planning was underway to create a scaled-down version of Chicora Park, and work started at the new site even in the shadow of the "brown skeleton of the Cotton Palace." By spring of 1903, the exposition had been largely cleared away, and "out of the wreckage and chaos has been created a garden like unto Eden."[81] The walks and flower beds were a showcase for tulips, hydrangeas, lilacs and phloxes, among many others. In the Sunken Gardens alone were 1,400 new plants. One hundred maples and chinaberry trees had already been planted in the formal portion of the park. The day-to-day operations of the park were entrusted to J.J. Bean, who had been in charge of the agricultural exhibit at the exposition. A gang of thirty-five convicts was used to level the grounds for a pavilion where the South Carolina Building had stood.

On May 25, 1903, a suggestion was made to name the new park in honor of General Wade Hampton of Civil War fame. The Board of Park Commissioners met on July 8, 1903, and the following resolution was unanimously passed: "Resolved. That the Board of the Park Commissioners heartily approve of the suggestion that the new park be called 'Hampton Park,' and do earnestly recommend the City Council to so designate it." City council approved the name on July 14, 1903, and modern Hampton Park was born.[82]

Although the city had soon acquired over two hundred acres of property for a park, there was never a totally unified plan for the entire tract. Instead, largely for financial reasons, Hampton Park's different portions developed in different ways. The Rhett Farm portion was always planned as a natural, countryside scene with winding roads. The portion east of Ashley Avenue was a much more active park with baseball fields, trolley hubs and other things. The central portion, also known as the formal gardens, was always planned as a passive park for strolling and the enjoyment of flowers.

The most popular portion of Hampton Park, and the portion that still remains intact, was the formal, central section around the Sunken Gardens. The first order of business after the city bought the land for Hampton Park was planting trees. Although a visitor to Hampton Park today might believe that the massive oaks have always been there, the reality is that after the exposition, the park commission was starting with nearly a blank slate: "This entire tract was destitute of trees when purchased and over one thousand trees have been planted along these walks and roadways, which will in a short time give the desired shade."

Since the close of the exposition, there had been no regular maintenance of the grounds, and the organizers of the exposition "endeavored to sell and remove from the grounds purchased by the city, everything of value." Some of the buildings from the exposition were still in place, but they were being torn down and hauled off. The city was unable or uninterested in keeping some of the remnants that had not been carried away: "Much of the [exposition] construction was of a temporary character, and had to be removed." Even into spring of 1904, clearing of debris was still going on at the park with a gang of twenty convicts removing the last plaster debris left scattered around the grounds.[83] The final clearing of the park prevented the park commission from pushing forward with all of its plans immediately, and instead, the commission mainly used the first year to simply secure and maintain existing features and begin the long-term process of tree planting.

One project that was undertaken early on was the bandstand. An often-repeated claim is that the bandstand is the last remaining building from the exposition, but in fact, that is incorrect. The bandstand remained from the exposition, but it had to be "remodeled and rebuilt." Instead of the original staff-decorated decoration, it was rebuilt using wood and metal.[84] Over more than a century, the bandstand has been rebuilt on several occasions (starting in 1906) and relocated twice. It was first moved and rebuilt in 1925, when it was relocated seventy-five feet westward of its original position at the northern end of the lagoon to make way for a sundial. Until that time it had had major work done to it, but it had remained in its original spot.

The Sunken Gardens portion of Hampton Park was a true island built in the middle of a shallow pond with bridges from each side. Like the rest of the exposition improvements, the bridges to the Sunken Gardens did not last long before having to be rebuilt in plainer style using more permanent concrete. *Margaretta Childs Archives, Historic Charleston of Foundation collection.*

The current bandstand, while a popular resting spot for park users and the location of many summer weddings, has no historical materials left in it.

A few other buildings lasted for a while after the close of the exposition. The Philadelphia Building, the Machinery Building and the railway depot stood for several years, but eventually the weather won out. The Maryland Building lasted until June 1913, when a suspicious fire destroyed it.[85] The Fine Arts Building was a solid masonry building that was far more permanent than its neighbors; it lasted until 1929, when it was dismantled and its bricks were salvaged by Eugene Schmetzer.[86]

The statuary from the exposition, however, was saved, and the park commission apparently envisioned keeping the temporary artworks as long as possible as a focal point: "The statutes on these grounds have been put in order and every endeavor will be made to preserve them." The Spanish pergola that ran along the inside curve of the main exhibition halls around the Sunken Gardens was saved for a time, and the statues were relocated there.

One building does, however, remain from the exposition. Located in the northeast corner of the exposition was a frame building with a gambrel roof and wood siding known as the Colonial Farm House. The building

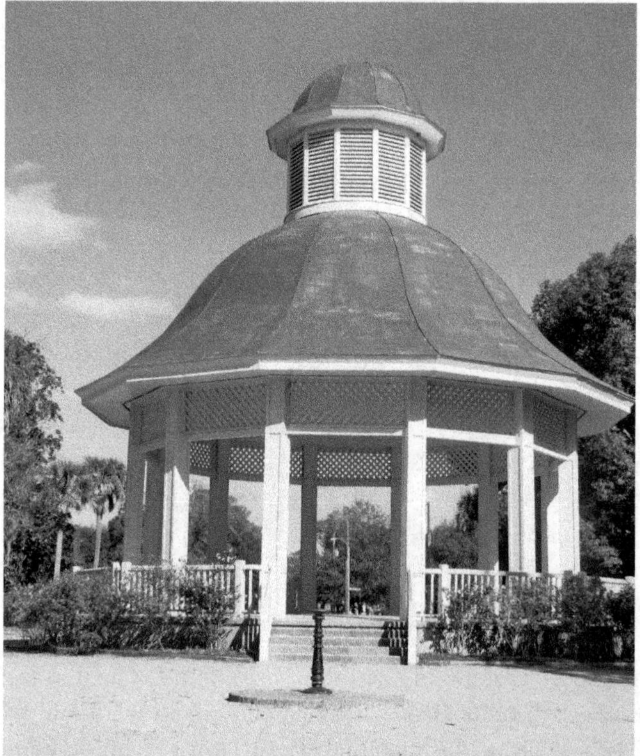

This page: The original bandstand for the exposition shares a general form with the current version, but its details were much more exuberant. Since 1902, the bandstand has been repaired and rebuilt frequently and even relocated twice. *Above: From promotional materials for the South Carolina Interstate and West Indian Exposition. Left: Photo by Julie Scofield.*

For a short time, the city tried to keep the staff statues from the exposition in good repair and used them as focal points in its new park. Eventually, weather won out, and the statues were removed by 1906. *Collection of the author.*

was operated by Mrs. Emma Brinton as a restaurant serving "old-fashioned cooking." Although the entrance has been modified, the quaint building is still intact at 30 Mary Murray Boulevard.[87]

Because building a public park from scratch was an enormous undertaking, efforts were concentrated on the Sunken Gardens, and other areas were ignored or used for other purposes. For example, one side effect of the exposition was the start of the Clemson Agricultural Experiment Station, today located south of Charleston on Highway 17. During the exposition, some of the grounds were set aside for the United States Department of Agriculture. Following the exposition, the city offered the land to the Agricultural Society of South Carolina for test crops, and the society began plantings in 1903. Standard cover crops like alfalfa, clover and grasses were grown, along with more surprising choices like peanuts, tobacco, cantaloupes and cotton, at times. In 1905, farmers were encouraged to ride to Hampton Park to learn about the variety of possible crops for the area and better farming practices.[88] By 1907, the activities had outgrown the Hampton Park site, and the society's testing grounds, already

This page: The only building still standing from the exposition is not the bandstand, but the much less flashy Colonial Inn. The unusual red building somehow survived the demolition process and was used for many years as a residence for the groundskeeper of Hampton Park. Since 1976, the building has been used by the city as offices for the parks department. *Left: From promotional materials for the South Carolina Interstate and West Indian Exposition. Below: Photo by author.*

being operated by Clemson College, moved to the country, about three miles outside Summerville.[89]

Some new buildings and improvements were being considered for the outlying areas of the park, including a dancing pavilion, a summer theater and a restaurant. Some of the new attractions were to be built by the Consolidated Railway, the company that operated the trolley lines. The relationship was symbiotic, to be sure; the railway company needed incentives to justify building a loop to the park, and the city wanted the loop to the park to increase visitors. Once completed, the railway charged only

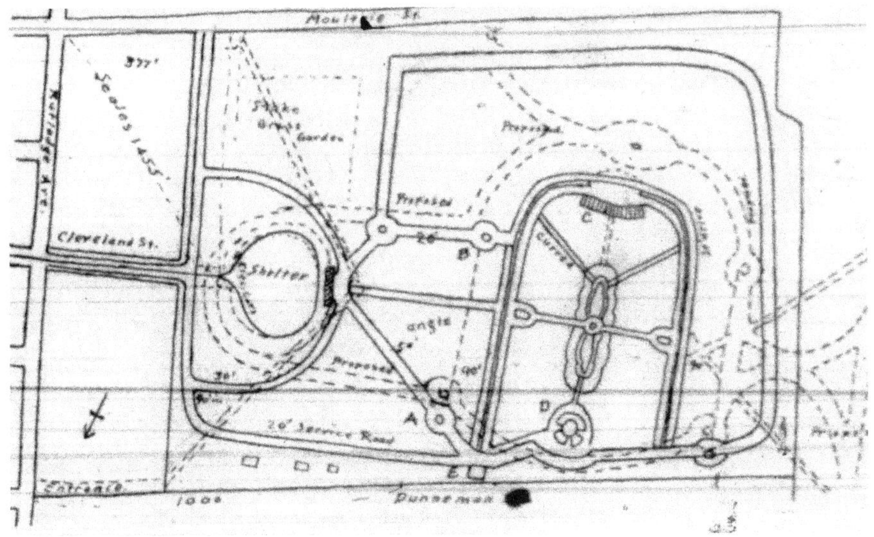

John Olmsted visited Charleston in 1906 to survey his canvas for the newly created Hampton Park. During his visits to the grounds, he sketched this rudimentary map showing a small plot for experimental agricultural in the upper left corner near Ashley Avenue. *Olmsted papers, Library of Congress.*

five cents for a trip to the park from downtown, and the easy, cheap access certainly was responsible for the popularity of a park. The first trolley runs to Hampton Park on the new loop took place on September 10, 1903.[90]

The only one of those improvements that ended up being built was the summer theater. The structure had a retractable canvas roof, a large stage, electric fans and seating for up to 1,200 people. From 1908 until the mid-1910s, the theater hosted traveling theater companies that would normally arrive in late May and put on a series of plays throughout the summer before moving on in August. Considering the summer weather in Charleston, it is doubtful that the theater ever actually lived up to the advertisements claiming that it was "as cool as a refrigerator car." Still, its productions regularly attracted several hundred spectators who enjoyed both the plays and moving pictures that were shown between acts. The Air Dome Theatre, as it was known, was located near the present-day intersection of Ashley Avenue and Mary Murray Boulevard. By 1922, it had decayed for lack of use to the point that it was condemned and torn down.

At least a few other features were added to the park that did not last to the present. In 1911, tennis courts were built and were an immediate hit

This image from 1907 shows the Hampton Park station for the city's trolley line located at the foot of Cleveland Street. Regular public transportation was important for the exposition and later made trips to Hampton Park easy and cheap too. *Collection of the author.*

The bungalow shelter erected in 1910 was, by the time of this 1944 photo, converted into a Girl Scout building. The charming building did not survive to the present but appears to have been located near the intersection of Moultrie and Kenilworth Avenues. *From a 1944 city report.*

with the public. Before long, there was a weeklong reservation list to play at the courts, and more courts were added in 1915. Also added in 1911 was a "bungalow shelter, complete with toilets, etc., for women and children."

In 1911, a proposal was made to develop a part of the eastern portion of Hampton Park into a more active commercial park instead of a passive resort. While Olmsted appreciated that a roller coaster might draw more people to the park and that the city could benefit from the 5 percent of the proceeds it would receive, his response was characteristically terse: "[W]e believe that the roller coaster would be such an exceedingly conspicuous and hideous construction, judging from those we have seen elsewhere, that the disfigurement to the park would be all out of proportion to the above advantages."[91]

Another portion of Hampton Park that was used for a different purpose for at least the first several years was the extreme southeast corner. Today, the land is known as McMahon Playground and is a popular spot for summer softball leagues and soccer matches. For many years, the same spot was the home of a minor-league baseball team. The original South Atlantic League was formed in 1904, and Charleston had one of the original teams. In February 1904, the new team leased a corner of Hampton Park between Ashley and Rutledge Avenues and started constructing a new ballpark to replace the facility on Meeting Street.

The site was convenient for fans, but the grounds needed work. When construction began, there was still a ridge in the ground left from the old Washington Race Course that ran through the outfield.[92] Work progressed quickly on the field and grandstands, and the first professional game was held in April 1904. During the first season, there was no fence around the field, and a stray cow would sometimes wander over. But by the start of the 1905 season, everything was in order for play. Indeed, the Boston Braves (the forerunner of the Atlanta Braves) held a week of spring training at the Hampton Park baseball stadium. Over the next few seasons, the ballpark hosted other professional teams, including the Philadelphia Phillies and the Detroit Tigers (including Ty Cobb, who played at the field in 1906). Regular season games often drew crowds of more than 1,500 to Hampton Park, paying fifteen cents for a ticket to the game. By 1907, the area was becoming a hub of baseball, and the College of Charleston began making plans for its own field just to the north at what today is College Park. After a hurricane in August 1911 destroyed the professional stadium, the Charleston Sea Gulls relocated to College Park, but the earlier field was still used for some training.

Meanwhile, an almost entirely different park was planned for the Rhett Farm portion of Hampton Park to the west of the formal gardens down to the banks of the Ashley River. On July 14, 1903, city council approved the purchase of the Rhett Farm to extend Hampton Park, but it was leased out for farming purposes for several more years until the full price had been paid off. On March 1, 1906, a final payment was made on the $35,000 price, and the western acreage was brought into Hampton Park, providing for a waterfront park. Still, because of other pressing needs on the existing grounds, the park commission continued using the Rhett Farm as agricultural property for another five years and leased it out at $15 per acre until it could be attended to.

While the decision to lease out part of Hampton Park was financially necessary, the decision opened the door to the one scandal associated with the development of the park. The secretary of the park commission was embroiled in allegations of payroll padding, using city workers and equipment on private property and outright theft. He admitted planting parts of the city parkland with crops and selling them for personal benefit, but he justified his behavior by saying that his efforts kept weeds down on the land and enriched the soil through his fertilizing the fields. The secretary of the commission lost his job, but he fought the allegations for several more years before city council finally declared the matter ended.[93]

The residents of Charleston embraced the idea of a park on the peninsula. In 1904 alone, the city planted 2,500 trees and shrubs, many of which were donated by citizens. The donation of plant material continued the following year when, according to the 1905 report of the park commission, "over 1,000 tree have been planted," which, together with those planted in previous years, "will eventually give the shade required as when the tract of land now known as Hampton Park was turned over to the Park Commissioners, it was entirely devoid of trees." Chairman Lapham was able to use the civic-mindedness of Charlestonians in his annual report to slide in a not-very-subtle barb at the inadequate funding of the park commission and the redirecting of the income from the Rhett Farm tract to the general budget of the city:

> *Many donations of plants, shrubs, and trees have been made to this park and all donations in this line that the citizens desire to make will be appreciated by the Park Board, as the funds available are small for so large a track* [sic] *of land to be cared for and improved, and the City Council has seen fit to take from the Park Board their income and have it placed to the general income account of the city, in order that it may be available for the general running of expenses of the City Government, in lieu of for*

A wide, wooden pergola ringed the northern edge of the Sunken Gardens during the exposition. When it rotted away, a metal version replaced it and was planted with flowering vines. *Collection of the author.*

> *maintenance of the parks of the city to which department in all fairness and justice it belongs.*

Even before the park commission had hired a landscape architect to design the attraction, it was already clearly popular with the people of Charleston. In the summers, Charlestonians frequently spent their leisure time at the Isle of Palms; the trolley system ran that far, and the commute was not as difficult as one might expect. But when the weather started to cool, crowds returned to Hampton Park to enjoy the "quieter pleasure of this beautiful place."[94] The park had not, of course, been without visitors at all, and during the summer, the youth of Charleston visited frequently: "The many secluded nooks, the long shaded walks, and particularly 'lovers' lane,' hold many attractions for them."

By September 1904, there were already at least some attractions in the park, including "an excellent ice cream and soda water parlor" with "broad piazzas." Still, the newspaper was already reporting that the park commission had its eyes on clearing the Rhett Farm to provide broad vistas, as well as plans for other improvements. Even by 1904, the newspaper reported that a goal for the park was a driveway. Until then, only pedestrians had been permitted in the park, but "in a short time carriages will be allowed in the park, which will add much to the pleasures of driving about the city."

On June 13, 1905, Lapham wrote to Olmsted to ask for his price for preparing the plans for Hampton Park. On March 19, 1906, Lapham wrote to the Olmsted firm and advised that the city had finally purchased the land for Hampton Park. He asked about arranging for a visit to occur as soon as April 1, 1906, to view the site.

On April 9, 1906, John Olmsted was in Charleston to inspect the grounds of the new park. His initial thoughts, as recorded in the notes of his first visit, were tepid. He made notes of the rail line that served the area and the plain, tar walks through the Rhett Farm tract to the west. His private thoughts about the park commissioners were hardly any more optimistic: "Jeffords seems to be acting as designer and superintendent under Mr. Lapham, who is the only Park commissioner who pays any attention to this park and even he very rarely goes out there. The rest hardly go there once a year." During the final day of touring the grounds, the gentlemen discussed a price. Olmsted quoted a figure of fifteen dollars per acre for the design work, plus expenses and the cost of assistants.

On April 4, 1906, Chairman Lapham mailed a contract on Olmsted's terms to him for his signature. Until that time, the park commission had not made wholesale improvements to the park beyond maintaining it lest their work have to be undone to conform to the plans of whomever they hired.[95] The Rhett Farm to the west and other parcels to the east were still being actively cultivated.

The chairman of the park commission was, however, a steadfast supporter of the long-term vision for Hampton Park. Lapham wrote about the importance of the project from the very start. Lapham's annual reports of his commission are remarkable in the amount of personal conviction they display. Year in and year out, each department and board of the city filed a boilerplate report of statistics and not much more. The park commission, on the other hand, reflected a zeal for its work in Lapham's gushing prose and heartfelt entreaties for adequate funding, especially for Hampton Park. In 1906, for example, he included the following defense of the city's expenses on parks as an investment:

> *Parks are a necessity, not a luxury, and their advantages are manifold. Though not always apparent at first, yet they tend to increase the value of real estate in their vicinity, and add to the general welfare of a city. The*

> *expense to each citizen is only his small proportionate share of the tax levy for this purpose, while every citizen can enjoy the pleasure and recreation that parks afford which but few can otherwise obtain.*

On May 1, 1906, Olmsted wrote to Lapham to review his initial thoughts for the overall design of Hampton Park before setting about generating more technical drawings. Olmsted's first point was to encourage in strong terms that the city not sell off the northeastern section of Hampton Park above Cleveland Street where a baseball field was in place. The use of the space as a baseball diamond "can hardly be considered a proper feature of a public park," but he suggested that, in his experience, the sale would be regretted when an inconsistent use encroached. Instead, he encouraged the city to keep the land and possibly use it in the future for a museum.[96]

Another recommendation was to change the main entrance of the park. Cleveland Avenue from Rutledge Avenue was unacceptable because of the trolley car lines, which, while objectionable themselves, were perhaps a necessary evil for a while. In the meantime, Olmsted recommended that if Ashley Avenue could be extended from Congress Street to the park, it would be the ideal entrance. Indeed, the city, he believed, should develop that entrance to give "dignity and amplitude" to the entrance.[97]

Olmsted was not the first person to note the unattractive entrance to the park from Rutledge Avenue; the poor condition of the entrance to the park had been a sore point for at least a few years. One citizen was quoted in a newspaper account pointing out the problem:

> [T]*he City of Charleston has apparently given no attention whatsoever to the appearance of that portion of the park that joins or fronts on Rutledge* [A]*venue. Instead of having this part of the park beautiful and attractive, inviting a visit from the passer-by, it is most forbidding. The rough, uninviting outlook with not a sign of improvements anywhere certainly don't seem to indicate the entrance to a city park. There isn't even a road or a path to get across to the place where the Exposition buildings stood. What was at one time a roadway seems now to have been taken up for a double line of car tracks, with an unsightly forest of trolley poles.*[98]

Olmsted noted that the bandstand was still in place in the formal gardens and should be highlighted since it was such a notable presence in the gardens. However, because large crowds might destroy the flowers he envisioned, he suggested that its use for music be ended. In addition, because the park was so wide, Olmsted suggested having a cross street along the western edge of the park. He suggested extending Hester Street, having the road cross the park and then running a new road diagonally to the corner of President and Congress Streets.

A speedway was a popular diversion in public parks of the day, and the straightaway along Moultrie Street and across the Rhett Farm would have been a fine half-mile run, but its location would eventually interfere with the burgeoning population south of the park and with the appearance of the park in general. Instead, Olmsted suggested that, if the city could acquire the Dunnemann Tract to the north, a long raceway could be added there with only one entrance from the north of the park. After all, he noted, "[t]here would never be more than a comparatively small population north of the Park…"

Other advice included potentially building a shallow boating channel south of the Rhett Farm, completing a drive from Spring Street along the western shore of the park and acquiring and filling the marsh southwest of the park to prevent the intrusion of industrial uses that would block the riverfront views. The notion of a vaudeville theater or such establishment, built by the trolley system, was totally objectionable to the planners.

Although the collection of ideas reveals much about the Olmsted vision for Hampton Park, none of the suggestions was taken. Of those that were even partially acted upon, most have been completely erased from the landscape. The baseball field north of Cleveland Street was eventually sold to The Citadel, no boating channel was ever dug, the main entrance remained on Cleveland Street, the Ashley Avenue entrance was never ornamented in any way, no direct cut-through road was built across the park, a vaudeville theater was built in the park, the marshlands southwest were completely built out with view-obstructing structures, the bandstand was not just retained but also specifically used for musical performances and Dunneman's land was never even acquired at all.

At the same time Lapham was working on the details of Hampton Park, Charleston's Mayor Rhett was making plans for Hampton Park as part of a larger development plan. Mayor Rhett, like Lapham, was a "big picture" politician with big plans for urban development of Charleston. His vision for the city was perhaps the first time a long-term plan for a comprehensive development scheme was thought out. In 1908, the city again turned to the Olmsted landscaping firm, but the city wanted more than just thoughts on a specific park. Mayor Rhett wrote to the Olmsted firm on April 11, 1908, and explained the true scope of what he and the city were proposing:

I do not know that you quite understand our purpose, which is to formulate a plan upon the lines of which the City is to be developed in the future. You know we are situated on a narrow Peninsular [sic], *which is fringed by large areas of marsh tracts. The time is coming, and we think it will come very shortly, when there will be rapid development and growth. What we want to do is to lay our lines so that this growth may be made to the best advantage, utilizing the space to the best commercial advantage, laying our Avenues and Parks, setting aside districts for residences with such restrictions as may be advisable, and altogether planning for a City of say 300,000 to 400,000 inhabitants.*[99]

Mayor Rhett hoped to develop the Ashley River side of the peninsula by filling the marshland and extending regular streets. The area south of Broad Street and west of King Street is largely landfill that was completed in the early twentieth century and sold off. The original plans, however, called for that same treatment to not just stop at the old Lucas Rice Mill (now the Coast Guard Station) but instead to solicit a major hotel for that location and continue the new waterfront boulevard all the way to Hampton Park. A rendering of Mayor Rhett's ideal was run in the Jubilee Edition of the local newspaper on January 1, 1910, showing Hampton Park as the northern terminus for a grand waterfront drive.

The creation of a northern terminus to a waterfront park around the peninsula came a step closer in 1910. The lease on the Rhett Farm, which had been generating about $1,000 a year, expired and was not renewed. It was the western part of Hampton Park that most clearly reflected the Olmsted approach to landscape architecture, and Chairman Lapham intended to carry out Olmsted's plans. The park commission's first step toward integrating the western half of the park was to begin making plans for the "establishment of roadways thereon, bringing into public use the grove of oaks at the river side and a boat landing." The Olmsted firm did develop plans for the route showing that the west half of the park would remain a very open space with long, looping roads and paths connecting the formal portion of the park to the water. They were sent to Charleston on December 24, 1910. Even in February 1929, the idea of a continuous park around the peninsula was still actively pursued, but the impending financial crisis of later that year seems to have derailed those grand plans once and for all.

While most of the plans for Hampton Park were never carried out, it certainly was not for a lack of trying. Lapham was unflagging in his zealous advocacy for Charleston's parks, and Hampton Park in particular.

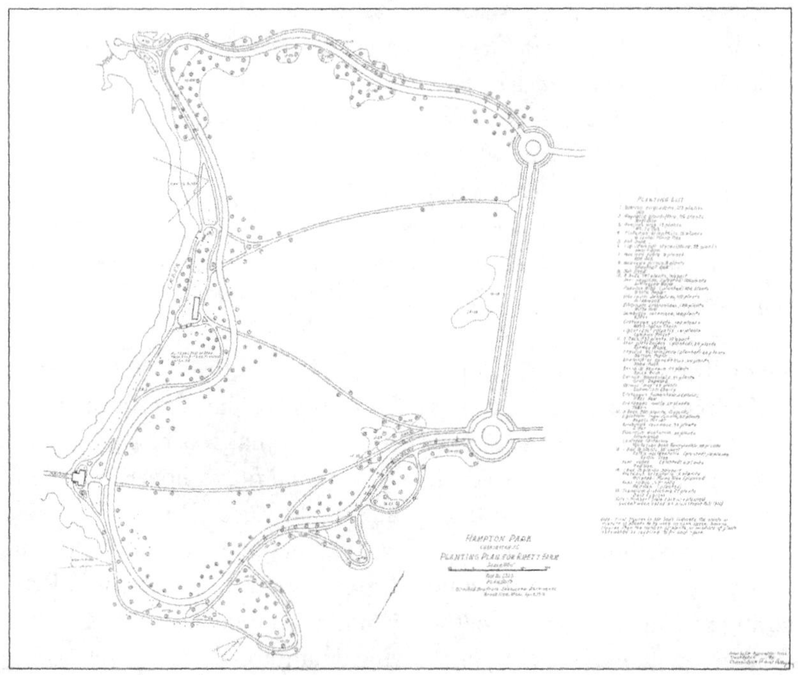

The main feature of Olmsted's plans for the Rhett Farm portion of Hampton Park was a long, looping driveway that would reveal sweeping views of the Ashley River. Although the western half of the park was sacrificed to keep The Citadel in Charleston, the route of Olmsted's drive remains as Hammond Avenue, Register Road and Richardson Avenue on the campus. *Plat from the Olmsted papers, on file at the Frederick Law Olmsted National Historic Site.*

> *The municipal allowances for parks, their maintenance, adornment and improvement should not be considered an appropriation but regarded as an investment, as it can be shown that every dollar expended for this purpose is returned by increased valuation of the taxable property of the city, and it is only by gradual and persistent effort in park work that our parks will eventually be worthy of our city.*

City council funded Hampton Park's operating costs every year, and the funds were used for extensive tree and flower plantings and maintenance. However, one project stood out to Lapham that needed a special allocation of public funds. In the early twentieth century, large-scale parks were intended for viewing as much as for active use, and planners envisioned a role in the park for cars (there were 245 in Charleston by 1910). A complete park would have included roads so that people could take pleasure drives and soak in revealed vistas from the comfort of private cars. Every year, Lapham pleaded for funding to build a drive along the riverfront in increasingly plaintive terms. In 1913, for example, after having his previous requests go unmet, he included the following in his annual report to city council:

> *The residents of cities are mainly dependent on parks for their opportunities to enjoy nature and we all know that pleasant natural conditions improve our minds and bodies, and exercise in the open air our health, and for those reasons funds have been asked for the roadway and walk to the River side of Hampton Park, the portion which was purchased to extend this park to the river, and which is now practically cut off from the original park. The Board does not expect, nor does it recommend that the development of the river side of the park be carried out and completed at once, but it earnestly asks that funds be given to begin this development, as there is nothing that should appeal more to the support of the people than the improvement of our parks.*

As the years went by without funding for a permanent road, his annual requests began sounding more dispirited than hopeful. In 1915, he wrote:

> *The opening of a permanent Driveway along the River front at Hampton Park has been delayed from year to year, for lack of funds for this much needed improvement. This state of affairs should not exist, as a cessation of improvements causes the general public to grow apathetic concerning the welfare of the Parks of the City. This Driveway along the marsh at the river front would open up a pleasing vista of Ashley River and beyond, and add much to the attractiveness of this Park, as a Park should exist primarily for its scenery and its contrast to the city with its multitude of buildings. The pleasure, contentment and well-being of a people are greatly enhanced by having parks in which to congregate and enjoy the beauties of nature.*

In 1916, his plea was repeated:

> *It is doubtful if any of the schemes of park development will meet with more general and hearty approval of the pubic than this proposed river drive, with its walks. This driveway along the marsh and bluffs will command the Ashley River scenery with all its beautiful vistas and views, and in the*

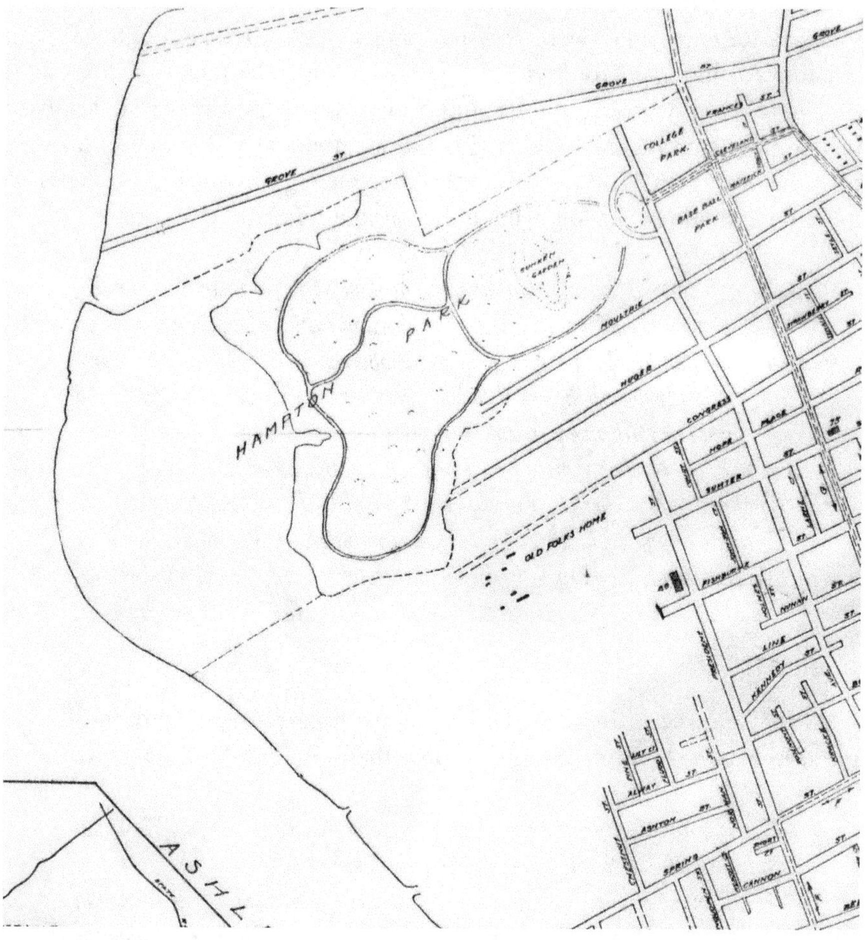

This map of Charleston was drawn in 1912 to show the vicinity of Charleston and its points of interest. By that point, the basic streets of Hampton Park Terrace were in place along with the looping routes of Hampton Park itself. *Charleston County Library, South Carolina Room.*

> *opinion of some of the most eminent landscape architects would make one of the most superb drives in this country.*

Although the funding was never allocated for a regular driveway near the water, maps of the period do show that at least a dirt road was laid out. In a map of Charleston from 1912, the Rhett Farm is already shown with the basic drives in place from the Olmsted plan from the previous year.

During his 1906 trip to Charleston, John Olmsted inspected the features of Hampton Park already in place. Since the close of the exposition, he wrote, the park commission had "laid out various drives and walks and their superintendent has planted them in the usual gardener's or cemetery style with hedges and rows of trees." The Fine Arts Building can still be seen in the background of this early image. *Collection of the author.*

On December 9, 1911, Olmsted delivered a set of plans for Hampton Park to his local representative, Leonard Macomber. Macomber arrived in Charleston in the winter of 1911 and remained at least several months, renting the house at 143 Wentworth Street. He briefly recapped the work that had occurred at Hampton Park and observed that most of the improvements were left over from the exposition.

Olmsted entrusted Macomber to take an active hand in deciding how to approach the long-term plan for the park. Olmsted, for example, raised the topic of the choice between heavy shade trees and hedges in their shade. Because he envisioned the park being used mainly in warm weather, the shade would be more valuable. In fifty years, he speculated, the hedges would have been abandoned, and it was better to plan on that eventuality. Other changes he asked Macomber to consider included tennis courts, a "hard gravel" playground for children and water basins.

As to the actual planting of the park, Olmsted was purposefully vague. He pointed out that the gentlemen should prepare well thought out but general

Starting with no trees whatsoever, it was important to begin planting where the exposition had been and also on the old Rhett Farm's pastures. By 1912, "several hundred young trees [had] been planted in groups on the riverside extension as set out in Olmsted Brothers plans." Today, the canopy of oaks along this central walkway from the bandstand to the Sunken Gardens is complete. *Collection of the author.*

plans that could easily be carried out in stages as funding became available. He emphasized that the plan should rely heavily on flowering shrubs and perennials, not annual beds. Perhaps, he mentioned, a few new formal gardens of dahlias or roses might be installed, but much of the land could be left to Bermuda grass for the time being. The overall effect of the plantings, he suggested, should be designed to be "decidedly interesting to visitors, particularly those from the North." He explained to Macomber that visitors flocked to the Drayton home on the Ashley River at Magnolia Gardens and advised him to visit there or at least read about the gardens. Without directly copying the designs of Magnolia Gardens, Macomber might develop some general ideas for laying out the grounds. For instance, he noted that a shallow channel might be dug out from the Ashley River along the swampy area and planted with cypress trees. Olmsted did volunteer that he preferred evergreen trees, red cedars and live oaks to the more readily available water oaks that the parks superintendent had been heavily using; because the streets made such heavy use of water oaks in the neighborhoods, he thought they should be nearly excluded from the park. Another disfavored tree was the palmetto "because they are not permanently hardy at Charleston."

While Macomber apparently made many of the day-to-day choices about the park, when Olmsted had a position on a topic, he was not shy about expressing it. When city council approved Hampton Park as the name for the new park, it also approved the placement of a monument to General Wade Hampton. The city did not pursue the monument itself, but the idea was not forgotten. On January 26, 1911, Louisa Smythe wrote directly to Mayor Rhett: "Eight years ago, it was decided by Daughters of the Confederacy to put up a memorial to Hampton—an 'Egyptian obelisk of correct proportions' on three low bases each about one foot high." The whole monument was to be about thirty feet tall, and Smythe wanted permission to erect it in Hampton Park.

Mayor Rhett and Chairman Lapham immediately forwarded the matter to Olmsted. The ladies had raised about $2,000, and the park commission seemed okay with a monument but did not like the shaft. Instead, they favored something more elaborate—an arch with a horse statute on the top at the entrance to the park at the cost of $6,000 or $7,000. The hot potato had been sent to the art commission, which sent it back to the park commission.

On February 18, 1911, Charles Valk, a member of the park commission, wrote separately to lobby Olmsted. He asked for an opinion after sharing his own: "I think [the proposal] more suitable for a Cemetery or some small park or circle. We have already several disfigurements in our parks, and think we should be more guarded in the future." On March 3, 1911, Olmsted wrote to Mayor Rhett with his perfectly clear opinion about the placement of a monument to General Wade Hampton. The snide tone of his letter bubbles through from the very opening, where he suggests that the backers could have made better use of the $2,000 they raised. He suggested that "I should have recommended the appropriation of fully half of the total sum ($2,000) for the employment of a designer of national reputation" to design a better monument, even if of "very small dimensions."

Olmsted knew the women had raised the money, but he stated they must not have spent much on the design: "[T]he design is one which can hardly have cost the stone contractor over $10, leaving $1,990 to go into material and mechanical labor." He had thought that the monument might have been appropriate for the entrance to Hampton Park, but upon review of the design, Olmsted not only could not find a location there, but anywhere else in the park that would be satisfactory.

Olmsted's objection to the inclusion of the Hampton monument does not seem to have been grounded in an objection to the particular design selected by the women but instead on a more general objection to commemorating war heroes:

> *Great soldiers are in effect great destroyers and their whole attitude towards affairs is one which is wholly out of harmony with all ideas and associations appropriate to landscape parks. The beauty of landscape, of trees and flowers and all that goes toward making a beautiful park, has nothing whatever in common with the activities and glories, the savage passions and ruthless destruction of valuable lives inherent to the practice of war. I therefore object to using a landscape park for sites to monuments erected to the commemoration of war leaders and to the glorification of fighting. I believe that such monuments should be placed either in the midst of the economic fighting and daily competition of the life of the City, where it should serve as an inspiration to courage and persistence and intelligence and the other qualities which make for success in this competitive world, or else in the place set apart for the monuments commemorative of the dead.*

Given the military background of General Hampton, Olmsted concluded his argument with a suggestion for a better location: The Citadel at Marion Square. In the end, the stone obelisk was raised along Meeting Street in Marion Square.

While the monument to General Wade Hampton was successfully avoided by Olmsted, another military monument was eventually added to Hampton Park. On May 9, 1910, Congress authorized the raising of the *Maine* to clear Havana's harbor. While the ship was exposed in a cofferdam in 1911 and early 1912, the United States had an opportunity to salvage some of its components. Dozens of commemorative plaques were crafted from the salvaged metal, but some actual items were also saved and placed in cemeteries, courthouses and other public locations across the country. The mainmast, for example, forms a memorial at Arlington National Cemetery. South Carolina's senator "Pitchfork" Ben Tillman secured at least two parts for his home state. A gun was installed at the statehouse in Columbia, South Carolina, and a capstan from the ship—a rotating post used to raise and lower chains or ropes on a ship—was given to the Charleston City Council in May 1913.

The precise location of the capstan's original display in Charleston is unknown. On July 16, 1927, the newspaper reported the relocation of the

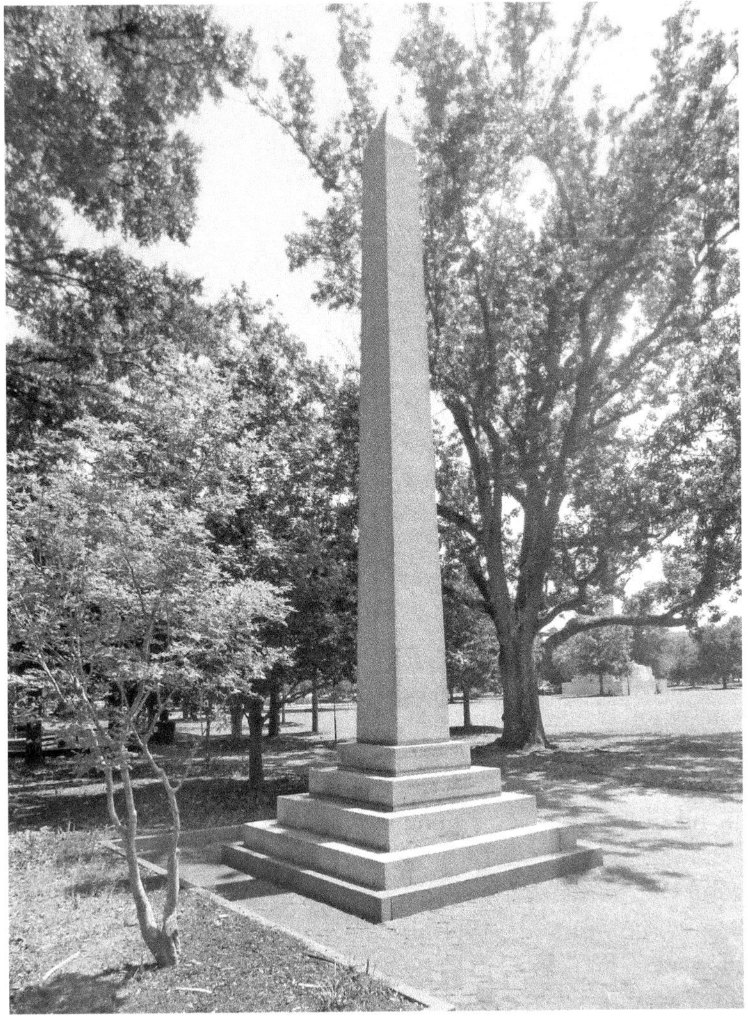

John Olmsted was at least able to offer one backhanded compliment for the design of the Wade Hampton memorial that was successfully diverted away from Hampton Park: "I must acknowledge that the design, if commonplace and uninspiring, has the one merit of being simple and not offensively vulgar as are many of the more expensive soldiers monuments." *Photo by author.*

capstan to White Point Garden from its home at the United States Navy Yard a few miles away.[100] The navy yard, though, had not been the capstan's first location. Instead, one speaker at the reinstallation ceremony proudly noted that the move had rescued the capstan from "such an obscure location" as

Rally Round
the Capstan
of the
"Maine"
at
Charleston, S. C.
in
1924

This postcard from 1924 depicts the capstan of the *Maine* at the United States Navy base after having been removed from its first location in Hampton Park to make way for The Citadel's new campus. *Collection of the author.*

the western end of Hampton Park. Likely, the capstan had been installed in Hampton Park in 1913 and remained until The Citadel relocated to the spot in 1922, when it was sent to the navy yard.

Even more intrusive than military monuments was an actual military camp created in 1917. To assist in war activities, a two-acre portion of Hampton Park was leased to the U.S. Quartermaster's Department for stables, and a campsite was furnished for the Headquarters Company of the U.S. Seventeenth Infantry. The military remained for two years. When the army decamped, the city was left with their stables. And while Olmsted would have been aghast at the use of the park for a military encampment, the city at least received all of the manure it could use for soil improvements from the army's stables, according to the 1918 report on Hampton Park.

Chapter 9
THE CITADEL

The worst setback for Hampton Park occurred just as the park was maturing. The Citadel, the state's military college, had been located on Marion Square for nearly eighty years. Growth of the school and the condition of its buildings made a move inevitable, and Charleston wanted to keep the school. After other options in the Upstate were considered, Charleston agreed to donate the western part of Hampton Park to the school for use as its new campus. The campus would include about eighty acres of highland and another one hundred acres of reclaimable marsh.[101]

While the city perhaps made the correct decision to donate part of its park to the state to keep The Citadel in Charleston, the decision was certainly not without its critics. Most notably, Chairman Lapham, who for so long had championed the cause of a waterfront park with a riverfront drive, sounded upset but still hopeful that the campus could be part of the public realm in his 1918 report:

> *The donation of the River Tract of Hampton Park to the State for the site for the South Carolina Military Academy, (Citadel), reduces the area of Hampton Park about one-half, but by co-operation of the State and City Authorities in the erection of The Citadel Buildings and the laying out of its grounds, with due regard to the park and its landscape features, the natural beauties of the park can be maintained. Every endeavor should be made to make the combination of The Citadel and the Park, one complete picture, and in this connection, the driveway around the entire area, now in*

> *construction, should be completed so as to take in the whole river front, with its superb river view, that this be not lost, as one of the enjoyable features of the Park. If the authorities of the State and City can work in harmony, then education and recreation combined, can make Hampton Park, more attractive, and its beauties be increased, not diminished.*

Today, the campus of The Citadel is open to the public, but it is surrounded by a chain-link fence topped with barbed wire. Two maps, one from 1915 showing the newly laid out Hampton Park Terrace to the south and one from 1918, show the impact of The Citadel on Chairman Lapham's dream of a riverfront drive.

In a last hurrah, the old grounds of Orange Grove Plantation and the Rhett Farm were the site of a final, remarkable event before being severed from the public park. On April 16, 1919, a touring company of stunt airplane pilots performed the first air show in Charleston.[102] The first airplane was flown in the Charleston area near Rifle Range Road in Mount Pleasant in 1911, but the novelty of flight was still an enormous draw, more so when stunt pilots reenacted battles and performed death-defying feats of derring-do. Schools closed for half a day, and many businesses shut down, too.

Planes arrived from Richmond in the morning on a special train. Eleven planes in total were shipped to Hampton Park in pieces, where they were reassembled. The planes had their engines and fuselages together, but the wings and other parts were bolted on at the park. Thousands of spectators arrived to watch the planes take off from a spot near Indian Hill. There were at least four Curtiss Hs, which took off in a northwesterly direction, turned back, circled around Hampton Park, sped over the city and then engaged in a mock battle including "thrilling stunts and turns," "turning loops" and a "daring nose spin." Machine guns were fired occasionally, but they could not be heard over the engines and propellers.

The entire show was part of a promotional tour for the Victory Liberty Loan program, and everything was geared toward spectacle. "Some flew so high that they were hidden in or above the clouds, and there were many exclamations of wonderment at times." At one point, a pilot even threw promotional literature out to the crowds below. The military aspect of the plane was clearly on display. The lead ace was Lieutenant J.C. Donaldson, "with a record of eight Hun planes brought down." While the planes were being put together, the crowd admired their "war camouflage and distinctive markings, and their many interesting devices." After the combat, the plan was to line up the "winged war instruments" for public inspection. And as

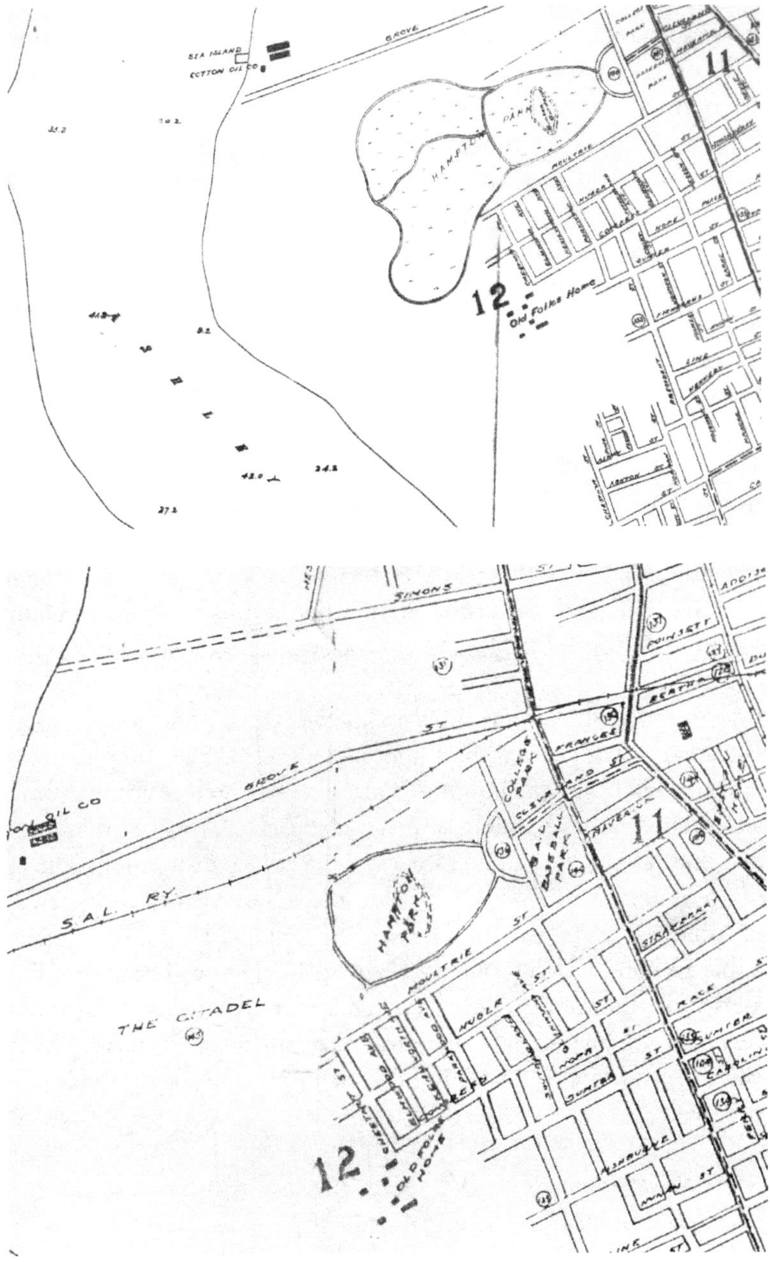

The relocation of The Citadel to the upper peninsula was necessary to prevent the school's move from Charleston. Hampton Park, however, bore a tremendous loss of land, with the entire western portion disappearing between 1915 and 1919, as shown in these city maps. *Charleston County Library, South Carolina Room.*

the newspaper reported, interest in the event was not confined to the boys and men of Charleston: "Interest in the part of the spectators was by no means confined to the machines, the aviators coming in for their share of curiosity, especially by members of the fair sex."

Charleston would remember the display for a long time: "It was an impressive demonstration of the battling power of the airplane." In one moment of hopefully unexpected excitement, there was a near accident when a plane, on landing, came in too low and clipped a telegraph wire in Hampton Park.

The cornerstone of the new Citadel campus was laid on Thanksgiving Day 1920 and had all of the pageantry one might expect. Samuel T. Lanham, the head of the Masonic lodge of South Carolina, laid the stone. To celebrate the occasion, he wore a piece of jewelry that the masons had acquired from the Marquis de Lafayette in 1825 during his South Carolina tour. Lanham used a trowel that the French general himself had used to lay the cornerstone for a memorial to General DeKalb.[103] A crowd of seven thousand celebrants attended the speech of Governor Cooper before moving back to Hampton Park, where the South Carolina Gamecocks defeated The Citadel's football team 7–6.[104]

Work on the new campus took about two years. The southern end of the Rhett Farm was cleared thoroughly enough that the campus was easily visible from neighboring Hampton Park Terrace, and a hospital, quarters and an administration building were soon started. A row of sycamores was retained that had been planted as part of the park construction. The cadets moved on September 20, 1922, to begin the school year in their new home on the Ashley River.[105]

Unable to complete his riverfront drive, Chairman Lapham refocused his energy on building at least a permanent driving route around the perimeter of the formal gardens remaining on the eastern side. By 1922, his tone in his annual report had become confrontational, albeit perhaps well deserved:

> *The Roadway around the Park is in a most deplorable condition, and is causing some very harsh criticism, and rightly so, the condition of this driveway detracts from the beauty of the Park, and some means should be found in which a permanent road could be constructed, which would add very materially to the comfort of the visitors, as it is now, it is a disgrace and reflection on the efforts of the Board.*

This early aerial view of The Citadel's new campus was taken in 1934. The remains of the riverfront drive can still be seen along the edges of the campus. The much-reduced Hampton Park is visible in the upper right corner. *The Citadel, the Military College of South Carolina archives.*

Christopher Werner crafted the decorative portion of these gates in about 1830 as window guards. Their first home was destroyed in the Earthquake of 1886, but they were salvaged and installed on a new building, which was bought by The Citadel in 1908. The Citadel took the ironwork to its new campus but later fashioned them into gates for the Aiken home of Citadel president Charles P. Summerall. After the general's death, the gates, still bearing his initials, were returned to the campus and installed at the entrance at the northwest corner of Hampton Park as the Summerall Gates. *Photo by author.*

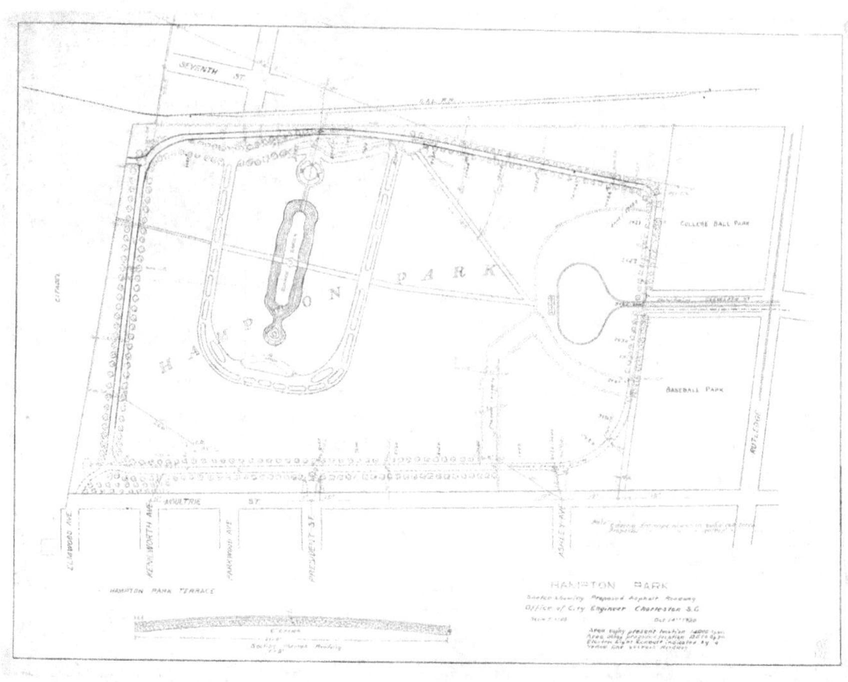
SEVENTH ST
HAMPTON PARK
COLLEGE BALL PARK
BASEBALL PARK
MOULTRIE ST
ELMWOOD AVE
KENILWORTH AVE
PARKWOOD AVE
PRESIDENT ST
ASHLEY AVE
RUTLEDGE
HAMPTON PARK TERRACE
HAMPTON PARK

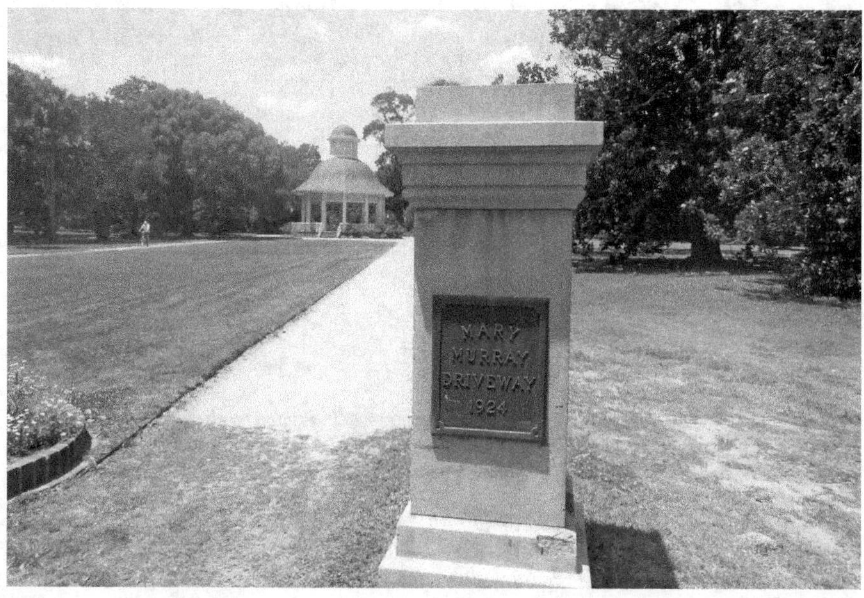
MARY
MURRAY
DRIVEWAY
1924

After nearly two decades of seeking money for road improvements in Hampton Park, the funds were finally in place in 1924. City council never appropriated any money for the purpose of paving the road around Hampton Park, and the money was instead donated to Charleston by one of its most civic-minded residents. Andrew Buist Murray had been adopted into the Bennett family and made his fortune in rice and lumber. In addition to generous donations to the Charleston Orphanage, the College of Charleston and local schools, he donated the $33,865 needed to pave the road in Hampton Park in April 1924.

Opposite, top: After more than twenty years, the road surrounding the heart of Hampton Park was paved to enable visitors to enjoy leisurely drives through the manicured gardens. The plans were prepared in 1920 by the city engineer but were not completed until 1924, when philanthropist Andrew Murray donated the money for paving. *City of Charleston archives.*

Opposite, bottom: In November 1924, city council dedicated the new road looping around Hampton Park as Mary Murray Boulevard in honor of Andrew B. Murray's wife, Mary Bennett. This photograph shows one of the two granite markers with bronze plaques that were installed at the end of Cleveland Street at the main entrance to Hampton Park. *Photo by Julie Scofield.*

Chapter 10

Decline and Rebirth

From the 1920s through the 1950s, Hampton Park served its role as a civic center for urban Charlestonians looking for outdoor recreation. During the 1910s, Hampton Park had drawn throngs of families looking for relief from a crowded, often dirty city, and Hampton Park enjoyed the backing of the city. Throughout the park's first twenty years—and demonstrating Chairman Lapham's commitment to Hampton Park—the budget for maintaining and improving Hampton Park typically was about half the entire park commission's annual budget. In 1914, more than 60 percent of the city's parks funding was spent in Hampton Park.

But things began to change in the 1960s. Both in Charleston and nationwide, families began moving to the suburbs, and Hampton Park was left without a vocal community of users to support its upkeep. The slow, steady decline of Hampton Park followed the downward spiral of one of its most interesting twentieth-century features—its zoo. Wildlife had been included in Hampton Park almost since the time it was opened. By 1909, swans were kept in the lagoon in the Sunken Garden; when a stray dog attacked them, the head gardener swore that he would shoot any dogs found in the park.[106] By 1912, an alligator pond was in place.[107] In a 1914 report, there was the first mention of animals kept at the park as part of an actual zoo: two pairs of hoot owls, a pair of prairie dogs, pheasants and a black swan placed in a twenty- by twenty-foot enclosure. Two years later, an otter pond was added. By 1929, the collection had grown far more exotic; that year, the inventory for Hampton Park included fourteen monkeys, two gray foxes, one red fox, one coyote, three parrots, two honey bears, five deer, three goats, six sheep, two peacocks, four owls, two pheasants, two fox squirrels, three raccoons and twenty-five rabbits.

Surprisingly, most of the animals were gifts to the zoo and not purchases; individuals contributed alligators, birds and even a lion. In 1937, Archer M. Huntington of Brookgreen Gardens visited Charleston and toured Hampton Park's zoo. He invited the parks superintendent to his home above Georgetown, where he presented him with $1,000 for the zoo, along with some monkeys and birds from his own collection.[108] In the late 1930s, the Works Progress Administration funded an expansion of the zoo, and the zoo was expanded again in 1962.[109] The trolleys to Hampton Park had been quite popular, but when buses replaced them, the 1914 trolley station was donated to the parks department, and it found a new use as an indoor aviary.[110]

Hampton Park was on life support in the 1970s. In the early days of the park, there had certainly been losses around the edges. The loss of the Rhett Farm to The Citadel was a hemorrhage, and the baseball field at the northwest corner of the park (College Park today) was removed from the park later. But otherwise, the city remained committed to the idea of a public park. For example, in late 1937, the Charleston school board was interested in buying the southeast corner of the park for a new junior high school. Thankfully, city council rejected the offer on the grounds that no park lands should be given away, and the school board built Rivers Middle School on upper King Street, a few blocks away.[111]

Hampton Park Zoo was a victim of a changing neighborhood, but it was also a victim of changing views on zoos. The Animal Welfare Act of 1970 went into effect on December 24, 1971, and a representative of the Defenders of the Wildlife quickly reported violations to Mayor J. Palmer Gaillard.[112] By 1972, the Defenders of Wildlife had begun a campaign against Hampton Park, claiming that it violated federal standards.

For the next three years, the focus of Hampton Park was on its zoo, but there was no clear direction. At least one councilman quickly suggested closing the Hampton Park Zoo and replacing it with a traditional recreational park with playing fields and a bicycle path.[113] But giving up on having a zoo in the park was not a clearly favored choice at the start at all.

The first plan for the zoo was developed by two college students. The city paid $500, and two students at the University of Georgia developed plans as part of their bachelor's degrees. The students were Lawrie E. Jordan and then unknown Robert C. Chesnut, a now notable Charleston landscape

Above: Anyone raised in Charleston before the 1970s is sure to remember trips to the zoo in Hampton Park. Bears and a lion were kept at the zoo in later years, but exotic birds were added to the park from the very start. *Opposite:* Eventually, the collection required a dedicated aviary, and the old trolley depot was later converted into a building for housing even more birds. *Above: Margaretta Childs Archives, Historic Charleston of Foundation collection. Opposite: From a city report.*

architect.[114] The total cost of those plans would have been about $300,000, and a nominal admission fee was discussed, mainly as a way to prevent wanton vandalism.[115]

In 1973, the Ways and Means Committee of City Council adopted the University of Georgia plans. As a follow-up, in October 1974, architect Frederick M. Ehni submitted plans that were far beyond what anyone had expected to implement those ideas. His plans called for moving the zoo, developing a better entrance at Cleveland Street and making other changes, which, some members felt, would stall the program for as many as five years.[116]

Another effort to plan a solution was developed by John M. Mehrtens, the director of the much larger Columbia Riverbanks Zoo. Instead of picking a single option, Mehrtens offered a variety of solutions. Options included closing the zoo, replacing it with a "mini-zoo" and completely replacing the larger zoo.[117]

In the end, no fewer than seven choices for the future of the zoo were developed in at least three different plans, but all of them were expensive. Retaining a zoo in Hampton Park was estimated to cost about $500,000 in repairs and then over $100,000 a year in upkeep.[118] The main cost would have been the complete redevelopment of the concept. In Hampton Park, animals were kept in small wire cages, sometimes little wider than some of the animals they housed. Across the river, in Charles Towne Landing, a new zoo placed animals in far more natural settings.

No one believed that the old model was appropriate, but the cost of upgrading to a new style and the acreage that would be required led more and more voices to support the closing of the zoo. *Charleston News & Courier* columnist Ashley Cooper added his voice to those in favor of closing the zoo in 1975. Continuing the old style of zoo was cruelty to animals, in his view. The rest of Hampton Park was little better. He quoted one woman who reported the state of affairs following a concert: "I was appalled at the mass of litter on the grounds. Not only candy wrappers, drink cans, bags, beer bottles, but actually raw garbage."[119] When city council finally decided to abandon the zoo, the newspaper eulogized it this way: "The Hampton Park 'zoo' is a zoo in name only, and has been for years. It is an outdated array of cages, enclosures and houses holding in captivity a pathetic collection of birds and animals."[120]

After the University of Georgia plan and the Riverbanks plan had both been disregarded, the parks department itself developed a third option. Like the others, its conclusion was that the existing facility was simply not working. There was enthusiasm among city council members to continue some sort of zoo, even a small one, but each plan was rejected when the costs were revealed.[121] The parks department's own plan was the final report, and it recommended that the zoo, except the birdhouse, be removed.[122] The parks board met on April 28, 1975, to finally pick a plan. During the meeting, one member summed up the sentiment of the body with this: "Hampton Park Zoo, as we know it, is dead. Let's give it a decent burial."[123] The parks board voted to close the zoo, and city council approved that plan in early 1975. The animals were removed and sent to Charles Towne Landing, and all of the cages were torn down except the aviary.[124]

At the same time the zoo was going through its final throes, the balance of Hampton Park was gripped by its own identity crisis. While the park might not have been neat and tidy, it seems to have enjoyed one of its more popular periods during the 1970s. There was a marked tension, though, between its youthful, active users and its traditional, passive park visitors. In 1976, a melancholy writer described his encounter with an elderly man in Hampton Park in an article that highlighted that tension:

> *His shoulders sagged despondently as he gazed successively on winebibbers among the rose bushes, romanticizers "making out" in the shade of the oleanders and clustered knots of listeners around portable radio sets blaring out "soul" music.*

> *He winced as the sultry breeze brought occasional whiffs of the acrid aroma of "grass" and his aging body successively dodged the touchdown efforts of youthful footballers and the often wildly thrown balls of those indulging in the one-time national sport…*
>
> *The constantly moving and changing press of people in the park moved backwards and forwards, sideways and sometimes upwards and downwards in a frenzy of unleashed energies seemingly incompatible with the sylvan serenity of the ancient trees surrounding the grassy areas.*
>
> *Beer cans, empty wine bottles, paper and styrofoam cups, empty cigarette packages and gum wrappers all cluttered the wan-looking and sparse grass sod that appeared to have been rooted up forcibly and was dying in the sun.*
>
> *The once orderly rose gardens, despite the protective thorns on the bushes, also felt the force of the heedless and overwhelming invasion of humanity…*
>
> *The raucous screams of the ball players mingled with the high-pitched whiffling of the soul music from the radios and a brisk sea breeze stirred the paper trash piled up under the azalea bushes.*[125]

When Mayor Joseph Riley took the reins at city hall, he publically stated his support for Hampton Park, which perhaps needed help balancing order and energy. During the summer of 1976, there were about twenty concerts—by the Charleston and Spartanburg County youth symphonies, the United States Marine Corps Band, The Citadel Band and Chorus, the Musicians Trust Fund group, the United States Navy Rock Band and others—but three of the shows had been marred by littering and disorderliness. He supported greater police presence and was committed to keeping Hampton Park safe and enjoyable.[126]

Very large crowds continued gathering at Hampton Park, and litter and public drinking continued to be problems. Crowds at the park typically reached two thousand to four thousand people and left paper and beer bottles scattered around. At one point, crowds began holding spontaneous musical events. When the city rejected one application for a disc jockey event, the city locked down the electrical supply box at the bandstand to try to squelch the gathering. Enterprising organizers brought a mobile generator to the park, and the event went ahead.[127]

Not only did groups continue holding events in Hampton Park, but the popularity of the gatherings also grew. Impromptu disco concerts drew as many as fourteen thousand attendees before, in April 1979, city council outlawed any organized entertainment in Hampton Park on Sundays. A special unit of the police department was stationed there on motorcycles and horseback to focus on marijuana violations and the enforcement of park rules.[128] The following month, Councilman Robert Ford asked city council to reconsider the ban, claiming that the city was "sitting on a time bomb" if music and dancing were not allowed.[129] Councilman Ford painted the issue as a race problem and stated that young black residents would demand a place to gather. His motion to return disco and dancing to the park was unanimously rejected by his colleagues.

At the park's lowest point, The Citadel—which had already been responsible for paring off more than one hundred acres of the park more than fifty years earlier—returned to the city. The Citadel wanted to expand, and it saw its chance to move eastward into the park. Its board of visitors developed a plan that would have transferred about 6 percent of Hampton Park's total acreage to the school for the construction of an auditorium and graduate school center. The newspaper editorialized that the transfer of the southwest corner of the park to The Citadel would be a mutually beneficial solution:

> *If The Citadel acquires and builds on it, the addition of tastefully designed structures could give impetus to a general revitalization that Hampton Park needs.*
>
> *Hampton Park is no longer what it was. For lack of attention, or whatever reason, it isn't a seasonal focal point for floral beauty anymore. It isn't a place where citizens of all ages can stroll or sit in the sun or otherwise enjoy peace and quiet because of the safety factor. Too often, street toughs, winos, and others from outside the law take over and scare away the law-abiding, despite all the talk about park rules and regulations.*[130]

As the newspaper saw things, the takeover would have salutary effect because of the "[e]xtension of Citadel jurisdiction, and the no-nonsense security associated with it."

In truth, the plans were even more shocking than the newspaper mentioned. While perhaps three acres of land would be occupied by buildings, the plan actually submitted by The Citadel would have removed ten acres of the park—more than 20 percent of its total space.[131] The new construction would have included a three-thousand-seat auditorium, a graduate studies center and an amphitheater.

Major General James Grimsley, who was then a vice-president at the school, appeared before city council on November 22, 1977, to argue that everyone would benefit from the plan. Some of the land would remain open

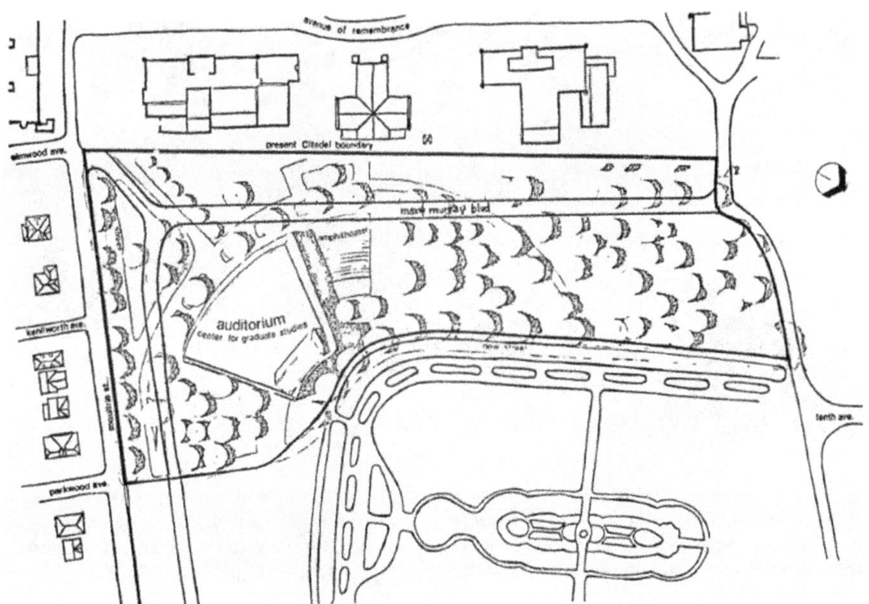

Because a large piece of the Mary Murray Avenue loop would have been lost, the plans submitted by The Citadel called to reroute a road through the middle of the park; a new road would have connected Parkwood Avenue on the south to Tenth Avenue on the north, running within feet of the paths around the Sunken Gardens. *The Citadel, the Military College of South Carolina archives.*

to the public as a park, and The Citadel had no current plans to develop that space. He suggested that The Citadel would gain much-needed room and actually remarked that the park would be *enhanced* by having a new auditorium built in it. It was a plan "in which everyone wins," the general said.

Not surprisingly, the public did not share the school's upbeat views. Neighbors from both adjacent neighborhoods, Hampton Park Terrace to the south and Wagener Terrace to the north, appeared and spoke against the plans. Giving up so much space was just a foothold for the school, they feared: "[W]hy not acquire the rest of it?" asked one opponent. In the end, the city opted to save the park. Funds had been spent on a master plan for the park, and the improvements were expected to start soon. "We're not throwing in the towel on Hampton Park," said Mayor Riley.

In 1980, the city started looking for money for the refurbishing of the park. The city applied repeatedly to the federal Urban Park and Recreation Recovery program for money to make expensive upgrades. A third

The unswerving commitment of Mayor Joseph P. Riley Jr. to urban green spaces was largely responsible for preventing the loss of Hampton Park in the 1980s. A plaque on a stone marker and a semicircle of park benches overlooking the fountain in the Sunken Gardens was added to celebrate his thirtieth anniversary as the mayor of Charleston. *Photo by author.*

application, seeking $425,000, would have funded plumbing and drainage repairs, electrical and lighting work, laying new grass, repaving the basketball courts, building of picnic shelters and fixing paths, among other projects.[132] When the federal funding for the program was drying up, city officials recognized that they might need to look elsewhere.[133] In July 1980, the third time proved to be the charm, and Mayor Riley held a press conference announcing that the city had been awarded a $425,000 federal grant, which it matched with $189,000 from a federal community development project.[134] In February 1981, city council awarded the contracts for the redesign of Hampton Park at its February 10 meeting.

In 1984, the work to Hampton Park was completed. The improvements included moving the bandstand to its current spot, adding parking and rebuilding the lagoon. The cost was $900,000. A special event was planned for the end of June 1984, and a ribbon cutting was held on June 30, 1984.[135] Earlier, on June 9, 1984, the first formal event held in the restored Hampton Park was the finale for Piccolo Spoleto, part of the larger Spoleto fine arts festival held annually in Charleston. With only a few exceptions, the finale for Piccolo Spoleto has continued to be held each year in Hampton Park, bringing out thousands of spectators to enjoy live music and picnics. Likewise, the MOJA arts festival concludes each year with a special event in Hampton Park.

The first special event held in the newly refurbished Hampton Park in June 1984 was the finale of Piccolo Spoleto, and the tradition has continued through today. *Photo by author.*

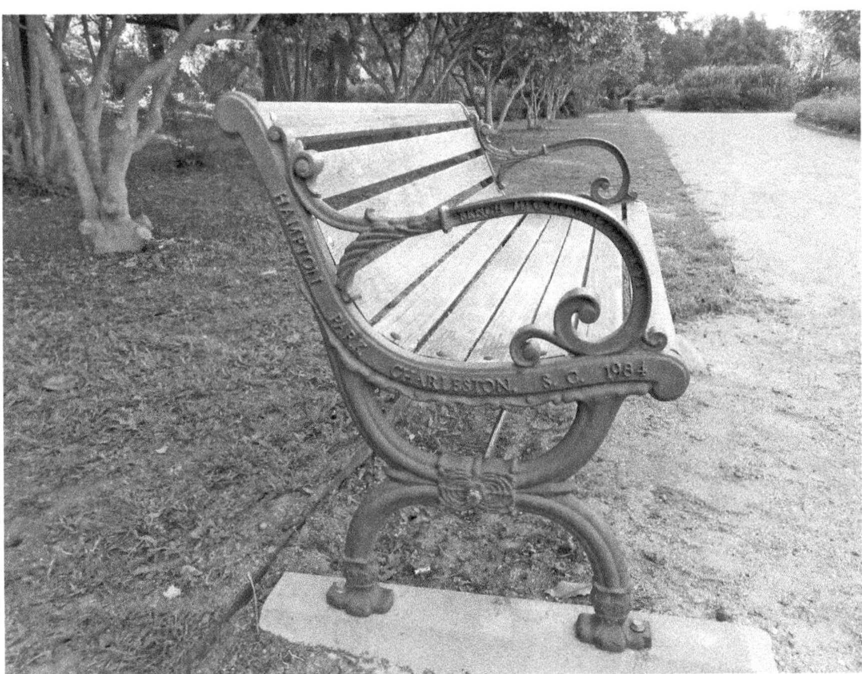

In 1919, there were over six hundred wooden benches in Hampton Park. Perhaps reflecting a more active use of green spaces, there are far fewer today. As part of the renewal of Hampton Park, in 1984 the city commissioned Battery-style benches with special wording cast on the legs to commemorate the work. *Photo by author.*

As part of the renovation of Hampton Park in the early 1980s, Charleston architect Sandy Logan designed a concession stand in what was described as "part Victorian and part pagoda-like." Linda's Hot Dogs operated out of the stand for a short time, and others have attempted to operate a snack bar, but no one has quite succeeded. It is currently shuttered, but locals use its patio and picnic tables often. *Photo by Julie Scofield.*

During the renovation of Hampton Park in the 1980s, the Sunken Gardens were greatly modified. A small island in the lagoon at the northern end still exists but has no public access or formal landscaping. A water feature still exists in an elevated pool at the southern end, but the fountain itself has been replaced. *Photo by Julie Scofield.*

Hampton Park continues to evolve. Along the northern edge of the park, for example, the city still has the stables and paddock that were used for the Charleston Police Department's horse-mounted patrols for many years. With the loss of the horse patrols, the city is considering uses for the buildings and might redevelop them into a venue for special events, such as wedding receptions. In the park itself, plans have been approved for the installation of a statue honoring slave-revolt leader Denmark Vesey, but the private funding for the artwork is still being solicited.[136] And in 2012, city council approved converting one of the lanes of Mary Murray Boulevard into a dedicated bike and pedestrian lane.[137]

For the last twenty years, Hampton Park has been on an upswing. Behind the old Colonial Inn at 30 Mary Murray Boulevard, the city operates large greenhouses in which the annuals for Hampton Park are raised. Every year, during every season, there are wonderful displays of plants of all kinds in the formal beds surrounding the Sunken Gardens. Along the western edge of the park, the city has developed a special, wooded area dedicated to native plants. In still other areas, the park offers broad lawns of grass that attract people playing Frisbee and sunbathing. All of the areas are tied together with an exercise trail that loops through the different portions of the park.

Today, Hampton Park is more popular than it has ever been. With effusive civic support and widespread use by many constituencies, its future seems solid. While it may never achieve the same fame as its cousins White Point Garden and the Waterfront Park, Hampton Park offers something for everyone, residents and tourists alike. Only minutes away from downtown Charleston, Hampton Park's fascinating history and physical beauty deserve a special trip.

NOTES

1. Gene Waddell, *Indians of the South Carolina Lowcountry, 1562–1751* (Columbia: University of South Carolina, 1980).
2. Charleston Country Register of Mesne Conveyances, Deed Book S, p. 251.
3. Stanley A. South, "An Archaeological Examination of Indian Hill on the Campus of The Citadel, Charleston, South Carolina" (1962). A copy of this excellent resource is available in The Citadel archives.
4. Bernard A. Uhlendorf, ed., *The Siege of Charleston* (Ann Arbor: University of Michigan Press, 1938).
5. Wilmot G. DeSaussure, *An Account of the Siege of Charleston, South Carolina in 1780* (Charleston, SC: News & Courier Book Presses, 1885).
6. Alexander Garden, *Anectodes of the Revolutionary War in America with Sketches of Character* (n.p., 1822), 269.
7. *South Carolina State Gazette*, legal notice, August 7, 1794.
8. *Charleston Morning Post*, advertisement, April 7, 1786.
9. *Charleston Evening Gazette*, list of events around town, May 16, 1786.
10. A plat from the South Carolina Jockey Club files can be viewed at the South Carolina Library Society showing the location of its new grandstands. To the northwest of the new stands, a brick house is shown.
11. *City Gazette*, advertisement, August 28, 1790.
12. John Irving, *The South Carolina Jockey Club* (Charleston, SC: Russell & Jones, 1857).
13. Charles Fraser, *Reminiscences of Charleston* (Charleston, SC: John Russell, 1854), 61–63.
14. Irving, *South Carolina Jockey Club*, 151–52.

15. "Charleston's Old Race Course a Noted Dueling Spot," *New York Times*, January 26, 1913; see also "The Schirmer Diary," *South Carolina Historical Magazine* 68, no. 2 (April 1967): 97.
16. "Journal of John Blake White," *South Carolina Historical Magazine* 43, no. 2 (April 1942): 114–15.
17. "A Statement," *Charleston Mercury*, July 30, 1856; "Col. Cunningham Dead," *Edgefield Advertiser*, March 23, 1893.
18. "Taber and Dawson," *Anderson Intelligencer*, July 11, 1889.
19. "The Affair of Honor Between Edward Magrath, Esq., and William R. Taber, Jr., Esq.," *Charleston Mercury*, October 2, 1856.
20. Arthur Peronneau Ford, *Life in the Confederate Army* (New York: The Neale Publishing Co., 1905), 14.
21. Warren Lee Goss, *The Soldier's Story of His Captivity at Andersonville, Belle Isle, and Other Rebel Prisons* (Boston: I.N. Richardson & Co., 1867), 193.
22. *Reports on the Treatment of Prisoners of War by the Rebel Authorities, During the War of the Rebellion*, Report 45, 40th Cong. 812 (testimony of Thomas A. Pillsbury), (1869).
23. Goss, *Soldier's Story*, 192.
24. Ethel Morse, "An Unofficial Memorial Day," *Journal of the Military Service Institution of the United States* 47 (1910): 111.
25. Granville Priest Conn, *History of the New Hampshire Surgeons in the War of Rebellion* (Concord, NH: Ira C. Evans Co., 1906), 288–94.
26. "Martyrs of the Race Course," *Charleston News & Courier*, May 2, 1865.
27. "Martyrs of the Race Course," *Harper's Weekly*, May 18, 1867.
28. "The Washington Race Course—A Generous and Timely Suggestion," *Charleston Daily News*, November 23, 1868.
29. "The South Carolina Institute Fair," *Charleston Daily Courier*, November 2, 1870.
30. "South Carolina Institute," *Charleston Daily News*, February 10, 1870.
31. "The Charleston of To-Day," *Charleston Daily News*, November 1, 1870.
32. "The South Carolina Institute Fair," *Charleston Daily News*, September 16, 1870.
33. "The Institute Fair," *Charleston Daily News*, November 6, 1870.
34. Ibid., November 5 and 7, 1870.
35. "Continuance of the Fair," *Charleston Daily Courier*, November 7, 1870.
36. "The Institute Fair," *Charleston Daily News*, October 25, 1870.
37. Ibid., November 2, 1870.
38. Ibid., November 9, 1870.
39. "New Better Monument," *Charleston News & Courier*, February 3, 1899.
40. "Racers to Winter South," *Charleston News & Courier*, August 18, 1902.
41. "His Life Crushed Out," *Charleston News & Courier*, August 19, 1902.
42. George Marshall Allan, "Charleston: A Typical City of the South," *Magazine of Travel* 1, no. 2, January 1895.

43. "The Old Race Course Gates," *Charleston News & Courier*, April 20, 1903.
44. "The Race Track Gates," *Charleston News & Courier*, April 21, 1903.
45. "Historic Posts for Belmont Park," *New York Times*, April 20, 1903.
46. "A South Carolina Exposition," *Charleston News & Courier*, October 4, 1899.
47. W.D. Parsons, "Charleston and the Exposition with Impressions of the South," *Inter-State Journal* (March–April 1902).
48. "Men Who Will Control," *Charleston News & Courier*, June 22, 1900.
49. "Mr. Bradford L. Gilbert," *Charleston News & Courier*, August 5, 1900.
50. J.C. Hemphill, "A Short Story of the South Carolina Interstate and West Indian Exposition," *1902 Charleston Yearbook* (Charleston, SC: News and Courier Book Presses).
51. "Laying the First Stone," *Charleston News & Courier*, December 12, 1900.
52. "At the Ivory City," *Charleston News & Courier*, November 19, 1901.
53. "A Leader of His People," *Charleston News & Courier*, September 12, 1901.
54. "Making an Exposition," *Charleston News & Courier*, July 28, 1901.
55. "Exposition Statuary," *Charleston News & Courier*, June 12, 1901.
56. "With the 'Staff Artists,'" *Charleston News & Courier*, June 30, 1901.
57. "Lake Juanita," *Charleston News & Courier*, October 2, 1901.
58. "Palaces Etched in Fire," *Charleston News & Courier*, December 8, 1901.
59. "Building the Midway," *Charleston News & Courier*, November 18, 1901.
60. "How About the Midway?" *Charleston News & Courier*, October 2, 1901.
61. "The Exposition Races," *Charleston News & Courier*, November 11, 1901.
62. "Exposition Races," *Charleston News & Courier*, November 21, 1901.
63. "Sunday at the Ivory City," *Charleston News & Courier*, December 9, 1901.
64. "Not Enough Horses," *Charleston News & Courier*, April 13, 1901.
65. "The Greatest Day of a Half Century of History," *Charleston News & Courier*, April 10, 1902.
66. W.D. Parsons, "Charleston and the Exposition with Impressions of the South," *Inter-State Journal* 4, no. 6 (double issue also marked as volume 5, no. 1 on the cover).
67. *City of Charleston 1902 Yearbook*, appendix at 119.
68. "The Last Night: Closing Scenes at the Ivory City Last Night," *Charleston News & Courier*, June 1, 1902.
69. "The Exposition Claims," *Charleston News & Courier*, July 15, 1902.
70. "For Exposition Claimants," *Charleston News & Courier*, May 30, 1903.
71. "Going, Going, Gone!," *Charleston News & Courier*, August 1, 1902.
72. "Exposition Furniture," *Charleston News & Courier*, August 6, 1902.
73. "Razing the Exposition," *Charleston News & Courier*, August 7, 1902.
74. "Tearing Down Buildings," *Charleston News & Courier*, March 29, 1903.

75. *1895 City Yearbook*, Report of John Adger, at 194–95.
76. Charleston County Register of Mesne Conveyances, Deed Book X23, p. 245.
77. Charleston County Register of Mesne Conveyances, Deed Book X23, p. 247.
78. *City of Charleston Yearbook 1901*, 135–36.
79. Ibid.
80. Charleston County Register of Mesne Conveyances, Deed Book X23, p. 514.
81. "Where the Ivory City Stood," *Charleston News & Courier*, April 30, 1903.
82. "Bete Noir of Council," *Charleston News & Courier*, July 15, 1903.
83. "At Hampton Park," *Charleston News & Courier*, March 4, 1904.
84. "A Trip to Hampton Park," *Charleston News & Courier*, August 14, 1903.
85. "Big Blaze at Park," *Charleston News & Courier*, June 30, 1913.
86. "Board of Parks and Playgrounds Ponders Fate of Relic of Charleston Exposition," *Charleston News & Courier*, November 24, 1952.
87. Robert Behre, "Building From 1901-02 West Indian Expo Survives, But Needs Your Help," *Charleston Post & Courier*, July 9, 2012.
88. "Experiments at the Park," *Charleston News & Courier*, May 6, 1905; "Inspected the Station," *Charleston News & Courier*, March 19, 1906.
89. G.H. Aull, "The South Carolina Agricultural Experiment Station," in circular 44 (December 1930): 24–28.
90. "Now for Hampton Park," *Charleston News & Courier*, September 10, 1903.
91. Letter of John Olmstead to Samuel Lapham, November 25, 1911.
92. "Making the New Ball Park," *Charleston News & Courier*, March 17, 1904.
93. "Won't Reopen Jeffords Case," *Charleston News & Courier*, July 12, 1911.
94. "Out at Hampton Park," *Charleston News & Courier*, September 2, 1904.
95. "Plans for the Park," *Charleston News & Courier*, May 12, 1906.
96. Letter of John Olmsted to Samuel Lapham, May 1, 1906, 1–2.
97. Ibid., 5.
98. "Whose Business Is It?," *Charleston News & Courier*, September 2, 1903.
99. Letter of Goodwin Rhett to Olmsted Bros., April 11, 1908, 1.
100. "Maine Tablets Brought Into View," *Charleston News & Courier*, July 16, 1927.
101. "Citadel Moves to New Plant," *State* [Columbia, SC], September 17, 1922.
102. "Flying Circus in Local Skies," *Charleston Evening Post*, April 15, 1919; "Flying Circus Attracts Gaze of Thousands to Watch Battle in Clouds," *Charleston Evening Post*, April 16, 1919.
103. "Citadel Readies for Great Day," *State* [Columbia, SC], November 9, 1920.
104. "Cornerstone Laid for New Citadel," *State* [Columbia, SC], November 26, 1920.
105. "Making Progress at Greater Citadel," *State* [Columbia, SC], November 20, 1921.
106. "Dogs Kill Lovely Swans," *Charleston News & Courier*, April 27, 1909.

107. "'Gator at Hampton Park," *Charleston News & Courier*, July 7, 1912.
108. "Huntington Gives Park Zoo $1000," *Charleston News & Courier*, May 29, 1937.
109. "Big Animals to Get More Floor Space," *Charleston News & Courier*, August 3, 1962.
110. "Do You Know Your Charleston?" *Charleston News & Courier*, February 28, 1938.
111. Ibid., December 13, 1937.
112. Barbara S. Williams, "Zoo Conditions Don't Meet Federal Guidelines, Official Says," *Charleston News & Courier*, May 19, 1972.
113. Barbara S. Williams, "Councilman Stine Proposes End to Hampton Park Zoo," *Charleston News & Courier*, May 23, 1972.
114. "Park Plan Being Developed," *Charleston News & Courier*, April 12, 1973.
115. John A. Alston, "Zoo Entrance Fee Proposed," *Charleston News & Courier*, August 28, 1973.
116. Mary A. Glass, "Hampton Park Redevelopment Unveiled," *Charleston News & Courier*, October 29, 1974.
117. Henry O. Counts, "Board of Parks Receives Report," *Charleston News & Courier*, March 25, 1975.
118. Henry O. Counts, "Hampton Zoo," *Charleston News & Courier*, March 30, 1975.
119. "Doing the Charleston," *Charleston News & Courier*, May 1, 1975.
120. "A Good Goodbye to the Zoo," *Charleston News & Courier*, April 30, 1975.
121. Henry O. Counts, "Whither the Zoo?" *Charleston News & Courier*, July 27, 1975.
122. Henry O. Counts, "Board Submits Plan for Zoo Facilities," *Charleston News & Courier*, July 29, 1975.
123. Henry O. Counts, "Board Votes to Eliminate Park Zoo," *Charleston News & Courier*, April 29, 1975.
124. Henry O. Counts, "Zoo Demolition Is Started," *Charleston News & Courier*, September 4, 1975.
125. Jack Leland, "Hampton Park: Man Recalls, Then Winces," *Charleston News & Courier*, August 7, 1976.
126. Mary A. Glass, "Riley Committed to Hampton Park Safety," *Charleston News & Courier*, August 11, 1976.
127. Mary A. Glass, "Crowds Leave Hampton Park 'A Mess,'" *Charleston News & Courier*, June 7, 1977.
128. Robert Small, "Hampton Park Won't Face Music," *Charleston News & Courier*, April 16, 1979.
129. Jerry Adams & Markie Harwood, "Council Puts Curb on Park Activities," *Charleston News & Courier*, May 23, 1979.
130. "The Citadel and Hampton Park," *Charleston News & Courier*, November 4, 1977.

131. Eleanor Flagler, "Park Plan Protested," *Charleston News & Courier*, November 23, 1977.

132. Mary A. Glass, "City Seeks Funds to Rehabilitate Park," *Charleston News & Courier*, March 24, 1980.

133. "Cutbacks Endanger Hampton Park Grant," *Charleston News & Courier*, April 11, 1980.

134. "Charleston Gets Park Grant, New Leisure Services Chief," *Charleston News & Courier*, July 17, 1980.

135. Sandra Bennett, "Hampton Park Nearly Ready to Open Up with New Look," *Charleston News & Courier*, May 30, 1984; Terry Joyce, "Hampton Park Unveils New Look at Opening Ceremony," *Charleston News & Courier*, July 1, 1984.

136. "Memorial to Vesey Under Way," *Charleston Post & Courier*, January 30, 2010.

137. "Hampton Park Cycling/Pedestrian Lane Approved by Charleston City Council," *Charleston Post & Courier*, June 20, 2012.

Index

About the Author

Kevin R. Eberle and his twin brother, Patrick, were born in Warner Robins, Georgia, in 1970 to George and Dorothy Eberle. The family moved less frequently than many military families and, in 1978, settled in Hanahan, South Carolina, about fifteen miles from Charleston. Kevin worked as a licensed tour guide in Charleston while home from the College of William and Mary and graduated in 1992. He returned to South Carolina for law school at the University of South Carolina, graduating in 1995.

Kevin accepted a position with Rosen, Rosen & Hagood, a law firm in downtown Charleston; began practicing law in 1995; and moved to the Hampton Park Terrace neighborhood in early 1996. He became active in the preservation community in Charleston and served six years on the board of directors of the Preservation Society of Charleston. In 2004, Kevin started teaching at the Charleston School of Law as an adjunct professor and joined the faculty full time in June 2006, teaching legal writing and analysis to entering students.

Kevin lives in (and works on) his 1914 house overlooking Hampton Park, helps with his neighborhood association, volunteers with the Preservation Society, tirelessly hunts for early photos of his neighborhood, tries to keep both his 1980 Volvo and 1961 Mercedes running at the same time and annoys his friends with long-winded discussions of whatever historical research he is working on.

CPSIA information can be obtained
at www.ICGtesting.com
Printed in the USA
LVHW020945210723
752843LV00013B/9

9 781540 231703